REFLECTIVE
LEARNING

Theory and Practice

Deborah A. Sugerman
Kathryn L. Doherty
Daniel E. Garvey
Michael A. Gass

University of New Hampshire

D0061335

KENDALL/HUNT PUBLISHING COMPANY
4050 Westmark Drive   Dubuque, Iowa 52002

Cover photo by Seth Goodwin

Dedication

This book is dedicated to our students
who continually challenge us
to higher levels of competence as teachers.

Contents

🌳 Post-Experience (Props Involved)   57

Introduction

As a young instructor working my first several groups on the "teams course," I remember being asked to make sure that I debriefed the group members after their completion on the course. Having no formal instruction on debriefing and no real understanding of the goals and techniques, I ventured into the complex area of reflective learning. I clearly remember my first try at it. The group of junior high school aged youths had just finished a wonderful day of working together and challenging themselves in group-oriented activities. I sat them down in a circle and asked "So, how did you feel about that?" As you can imagine, I got nothing in response but blank stares. I started to sweat. More blank stares, no comprehension on their part of what I was trying to get at, and no real skill on my part to get them to understand. Now THAT was a learning experience. After I bumbled my way through and the group finally departed on the bus, I vowed to find out more about debriefing so that I would not have to put the group or myself through that experience again. It is interesting to note how my experiences are similar to others' in the field (e.g., Quinsland & Van Ginkel, 1984).

After working in the field of outdoor education for many years, I have developed an understanding of the theoretical underpinnings of reflective learning and developed a wider repertoire of techniques. As I teach undergraduate students the skills and art of leadership and facilitation, I am reminded again and again how complex it can be. As facilitators it is hard to make sure it all happens. The planning, logistics, preparation, teaching, watching, being aware of safety—sometimes can be overwhelming. And then to have to somehow pull it all together so that the participants can express what they learned from it? Sometimes, this is the part that is overlooked in terms of thought and preparation. The reflective learning piece of the experience takes as much planning and preparation as the rest of the experience.

While discussing the challenge of teaching the techniques of facilitation, my colleagues Dan, Mike, Kathy, and I thought how wonderful it would be to have a book specifically on reflection. It would describe not only the theoretical aspects of reflection, but also give the reader some concrete ideas about methods to use while facilitating and activities to implement. The spark for this book was lit! As a collaborative endeavor, we pooled our knowledge and experience to aid facilitators in the planning and implementation of reflective teaming experiences. The first three chapters deal with the theoretical aspect of reflective learning. Chapter One develops the definition of reflection and discusses learning models in relation to reflection. Chapter Two explains techniques used by facilitators and includes a model for facilitator feedback to be used in the field. Chapter Three discusses the ethics of facilitation, with guidelines for facilitators. The final section of the book is a compilation of activities to use in reflective learning experiences. The activities are divided into sections for easy reference. The first section includes activities that can be used before an experience or both before and after the experience. The second section contains activities that are used after an experience and are further divided into those that need no props and those that need props.

Our thanks go to the professionals who have mentored us along our paths, and to our students who continually teach us. Our hope is that this book will be useful to you and that it aids you along, your path.

Deborah Sugerman
University of New Hampshire
September 9, 1999

The Role of Reflection in the Learning Process

M any educational theorists (e.g., Dewey, 1933, 1938; Freire, 1984; Schon, 1983, 1987; and Lewin and Kohler (Sprinthall, Sprinthall & Oja, 1994);) advocate that learning is dependent on integrating experience with reflection. Though they all maintain that learning cannot take place without reflection, definitions of the reflective process vary. Dewey (1933) defines reflection as "active, persistent, and careful consideration of any belief or supposed form of knowledge in the light of the grounds that support it and the further conclusions to which it tends" (p. 118). Boud, Keogh and Walker (1985) see reflection as a cognitive activity where people, "recapture their experience, think about it, mull it over, and evaluate it." (p. 19). De la Harpe and Radloff (1997) state that reflection "includes the ability to be self-aware, to analyze experiences, to evaluate their meaning and to plan further action based on the analysis and reflection" (p. 1).

Although these definitions vary concerning the specifics of reflection, their themes provide a solid base for making important observations regarding the process and outcome of reflection. The sequential steps of this process include (1) reorganizing perceptions, (2) forming new relationships, and (3) influencing future thoughts and actions. The outcome of these steps is the ability for individuals to "make meaning" from their experiences or, in other words, to learn from their experiences. This process of making meaning is a significant part of the reflection process, yet it is often overlooked.

Viktor Frankl (1984) discusses the importance of people making meaning in their reflective processes in his book *Man's Search for Meaning*. As a prisoner in a Nazi concentration camp, Frankl observed that those prisoners who made meaning of their experiences and were hopeful ultimately survived. Those who were not able to find meaning in their lives and who lost faith in the future died. He tells a story about one particularly dreary night when he was asked to talk about hope. He talked about the future, the past, survival, sacrifice, and the many opportunities of giving life meaning. As he talked, the men thought about their own lives and past and present experiences. "The purpose of my words was to find a full meaning in our life, then and there, in that hut and in that practically hopeless situation. I saw that my efforts had been successful . . . I saw the miserable figures of my friends limping toward me to thank me with tears in their eyes." (p. 91). These men were able to make meaning of their experiences and to learn from them, which influenced their future thoughts and actions.

Aldous Huxley talks about experience not as what happens to people, but what people do with what happens to them (Conrad & Hedin, 1991). Boyd and Fales (1983) also stress the importance of reflection and making meaning of experiences by stating that reflection is, "the process of creating and clarifying the meaning of experience (present or past) in terms of self" (p. 101). The connection between experience, reflection, making meaning, and learning is clear. Reflection is an essential part ·of the learning process because it can result in extracting meaning from the experience.

Learning Theories

In order to utilize the process of reflection, it is important to understand the models and theories that support reflective learning. Increasing participants' abilities to reflect requires a deeper understanding of how individuals process and manage intellectual information. Several important theories critical to the reflective learning concept include active learning, constructivism, narrative approaches (Luckner & Nadler, 1997), and thinking process and capacity (Piaget, 1965).

The theory of active learning implies that learning is not accomplished through the static acquisition of information given from teacher to student, but accomplished by learners actively making connections between new material and previous knowledge and experience. The meaning of new information for individuals is based on what they have already learned from past experiences and is assimilated through active involvement with the information through experience (Luckner & Nadler, 1997). Similarly, the theory of constructivism is based on the belief that learning takes place within the context of current knowledge. Theorists believe that learning depends on active involvement in the learning process and interactive communication with other learners (Fosnot, 1989). The narrative theory is based on the concept that learning takes place through stories. These stories are created from experiences and give value to certain aspects of the experiences. The metaphorical connections of the stories enable the learner to sort the information, learn from it, and generalize it to other situations (Luckner & Nadler, 1997).

Piaget (1965) concluded that the ability to learn is a result of two related factors: thinking process and thinking capacity. The thinking **process** refers to the way in which information is obtained, organized, and analyzed in the brain. Gardner (1993) divided these thinking processes into categories recognizing that individuals vary greatly in how they process information. For nearly every teaching method (e.g., lectures, readings, case studies, primary experiences, etc.), some students will be more comfortable than others simply because the style of instruction connects favorably to their preferred thinking process.

Thinking **capacity** in learning is the specific potency of the brain. Relatively recent research on the functioning of the brain suggests that different parts of the brain are accessed for different kinds of learning by recognizing patterns within the myriad of information received in order to make meaning from the input (Caine & Caine, 1994). It was also found that some brains have a greater capacity for certain learning activities than other brains. The ability of learners to understand and make sense of a learning experience is related to the capacity of their brain. As learning becomes necessary and/or interesting, learners expand brain capacity by performing the intellectual tasks necessary to fulfill the learning demand. Learning results as the brain sorts out information and places it into patterns based on past experiences.

Learning Models

Learning theories suggest that recognizing patterns and making connections between new material and previous experiences is key to learning. Three models of experiential education currently exist that discern the importance of the connections between past, present, and future learning. These models are particularly relevant to reflective learning, as each recognizes the importance of reflection in the learning process and making meaning from experiences. One of the first persons to do this was John Dewey (1938), who provided the underpinnings of an educational philosophy that is based on experience and reflection. Dewey understood that it was the careful selection of experiences, linked with commitment to reflection upon these experiences that formed the basis for the acquisition of new knowledge and learning. The process he developed involved the steps of (1) observing surrounding conditions, (2) obtaining knowledge from recollection of past experiences, and (3) gaining judgment from these observations and experiences. Dewey's model of experiential learning is represented in Figure 1.

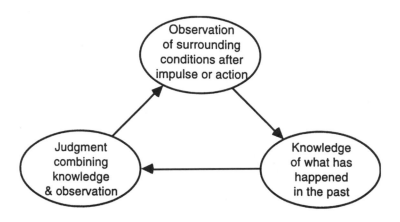

Figure 1: Dewey's (1938) process of experiential learning.

Reprinted by permission from Simon Priest and Michael A. Gass, 1997, *Effective Leadership in Adventure Planning*, (Champaign, IL: Human Kinetics).

Pfeiffer and Jones (1980) offered an expanded version of Dewey's model. Their learning theory was designed for group facilitators, but holds up well as a template for all learning. In their model (see Figure 2), the individual has the experience (Experiencing), shares reactions and observations with other group members (Publishing), discusses any themes or patterns (Processing), forms broad principles about how the world works (Generalizing), and integrates the learning into behavior (Applying). See Figure 2.

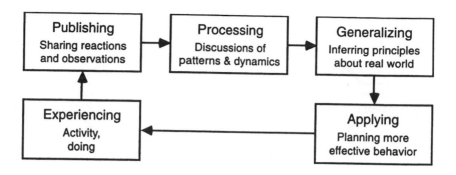

Figure 2: Pfeiffer and Jones's (1980) model of experiential learning.

Reprinted by permission from Simon Priest and Michael A. Gass, 1997, *Effective Leadership in Adventure Planning*, (Champaign, IL: Human Kinetics).

Perhaps the most often used model of learning theory associated with experiential education is David Kolb's (1984). Experience is the beginning of learning (Step 1). The learner encounters something in the world that must be accomplished as a task or understood as a concept. Following the experience, the learner reflects on what has occurred and gains clarity regarding the factual and subjective nature of the experience (Step 2). After reflecting, the learner generalizes by recognizing patterns of thinking or outcomes that have resulted from the experience (Step 3). During the generalizing stage the learner poses the following question: "In what ways were my thinking and the outcomes of this experience similar to or different from my thinking and outcomes following other experiences?" The learner attempts to form some consistent meaning about how this experience confirms or challenges previously held beliefs. In the final stage of testing in new situations, the learner uses the generalized new information obtained from the experience to make decisions about future experiences (Step 4). This cycle of experiencing, reflecting, generalizing, and testing forms the pattern of learning. See Figure 3.

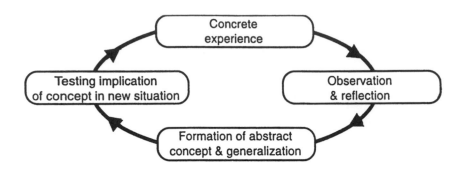

Figure 3: Kolb's (1984) interpretation of Lewin's experiential learning cycle.

Reprinted by permission from Simon Priest and Michael A. Gass, 1997, *Effective Leadership in Adventure Planning*, (Champaign, IL: Human Kinetics).

Encorporating Reflection into Learning

Based on educational theories and models, careful reflection is integral to the success of learning. Take away reflection and the individual has a series of experiences that are unconnected and ineffective in changing how he or she learns about the world. Yet theorists disagree on whether reflection is accomplished spontaneously by individuals, or if the techniques of reflection need to be taught. Several researchers (e.g., Atkins & Murphy, 1993 and de la Harpe & Radloff, 1997) found that many people do not appear to reflect spontaneously on their learning and suggest the skills required for reflection must be taught. Others (e.g., Oullette, 1991) state that educators cannot necessarily teach people how to reflect, but instead must facilitate the reflection process.

The content of ongoing reflection cannot be taught. It can only be guided through wise and caring direction. Since what reflection does is to . . . guide the synthesis of information and feelings unique to the experience of each individual, it is not necessary so much to 'teach' in an experiential setting as to guide learning. Carefully selected placements or settings for the learning experience will ensure the quality of experience. The task then, is to enable the learner to make the most of what has taken place by drawing the essence of the experience back time and again for nurturing and growth (p. 78).

Based on theories and models of learning and reflective learning, great care should be given to consciously incorporate reflection into teaching and to make the reflection activities varied and successful for participants. The facilitator enhances reflection and provides catalysts for learning by developing a thoughtful context in which individuals can extract meaning from their experiences. The use of specific techniques by the facilitator helps individuals sort information into recognizable patterns and make connections between past experience and current learning. Since reflecting on experience is the process that "opens the door to real learning" (Cairn, 1991, p. 77), providing the environment and opportunity for reflection may be the spark that lights the fire of learning.

Facilitation Techniques for Reflective Learning

P articipants who reflect on an experience are better able to extract lessons from the experience, to understand themselves in relation to the experience, and to apply the learning to other areas of their lives (de la Harpe & Radloff, 1997). Some participants are able to reflect spontaneously. They seem to understand the purpose and goals behind the experience and are able to connect themselves with those goals. Other participants are not able to reflect spontaneously on the experience and are unable to extract meaning by themselves. It is the role of the facilitator to set up an environment where learning through reflection can take place and all participants are able to understand the meaning of the experience for them. This reflective learning is accomplished through various techniques of the facilitator. The purpose of this chapter is to explain the techniques used by facilitators within the context of physical set-up, personal safety of participants, and verbal and non-verbal communication of the facilitator.

Physical Set-Up of the Reflection Activity

The physical set-up of the environment sets the stage for appropriate reflective learning. The group environment must be comfortable and safe in order for participants to reflect and learn. The location of the reflection activity should be appropriate for the goals of the activity. For example, if the goal of the reflection activity is to quietly reflect using a journal, it might be inappropriate to locate participants in the middle of a busy campground. The location should be accessible to all participants, regardless of physical or cognitive ability level. Outside distractions such as traffic, other people, insects, noise, temperature, etc. should be kept to a minimum. The location of the activity should be free of environmental hazards such as rock cliffs, dangerous beaches, or large holes.

The set-up of the group itself while involved in reflection must be appropriate for the goals of the activity. Care should be taken to ensure that everyone is physically included in the activity. Having everyone sit or stand in a circle ensures inclusivity and allows everyone to be at the same physical level. The location of any distractions is taken into account by the facilitator. For example, the sun is placed at the participants' backs. Any equipment or materials that are used should be appropriate for the activity and in good working order. The facilitator should be familiar with the equipment, and be able to teach participants its use.

The reflection activity should be appropriately sequenced within the learning experience. The facilitator should provide clear instructions concerning the reflection activity, and answer questions when asked. Appropriate structure should be provided, yet the facilitator should be flexible based on needs of the group and goals of the activity. Time management involves making sure that enough time is allotted for the reflection activity, and that the goals of the activity are accomplished within the time frame.

Personal Safety of Participants

The personal safety of participants involves both physical safety and emotional safety. Without safety measures in place, it is difficult for participants to commit to the reflection process. To ensure physical safety, the boundaries of the environment must be set and relayed to the participants. Any hazards should be pointed out and avoided if possible. Group participants should be prepared for the conditions within which the facilitation occurs. This may entail forewarning participants about conditions and checking to make sure they are adequately prepared. Facilitators should have appropriate safety equipment available, and be familiar with prescribed accident response protocol. The facilitator uses appropriate touching, with awareness of cultural differences and physical/emotional boundaries of the group. Emotional safety involves the "emotional boundaries" set by the facilitator and the group. The concepts of the Full Value Contract (Schoel, Prouty & Radcliffe, 1988) and Challenge by Choice (Rohnke, 1984) set the base for emotional safety. The specifics of these techniques will not be discussed in this book, but can be researched through the references. The ground rules of facilitation should be discussed with the group. Examples of ground rules include one person speaks at a time, no violence, no discounting, etc. The facilitator is the role model for self-disclosure during reflection, and should model appropriate disclosure and monitor the disclosure of participants. See Chapter 3 for more information concerning levels of disclosure. Finally, the facilitator should value the individual differences of group members concerning their safety in the group.

The Facilitation Process

When the group is involved in the learning experience, the facilitator's roles increase. He or she is assessing, watching, listening, and being aware of personal feelings. The facilitator constantly assesses the group and individuals in the group to evaluate their physical and emotional conditions and their current needs in the setting. Models such as the GRABBS model (Schoel, Prouty & Radcliffe, 1988) and CHANGES model (Gass & Gillis, 1995a) help the facilitator to assess participants. Facilitators have their "antennas up," watching what happens in the experience, listening to what is being said, and being aware of any feelings they have about what is happening in the group. This constant vigilance gives the facilitator information to help individuals connect the experience with reflective learning. As the experience progresses, the facilitator formulates a plan about important areas to cover in the reflection portion of the experience based on what he or she observes, hears and feels. The facilitator guides the individuals through the learning process using verbal and nonverbal behavior as the group is engaged in the reflection process. The actions and behaviors of the facilitator direct the reflective learning process to a successful completion.

Nonverbal Communication

The facilitator communicates with the group through many nonverbal methods including personal presence, physical positioning within the group, and physical attributes. A facilitator who has a presence of competence and confidence, in addition to humility and modesty, will communicate approachability and caring to group members. As previously referred to, the group should be appropriately inclusive when working on reflection. The facilitator should be aware of his/her location within the group, and should be at the same level as the participants. Nonverbal communication techniques such as body posture, facial expressions, eye contact, and hand and body movements should be culturally appropriate and intentionally used within the reflection activity.

Verbal Communication

The techniques of using voice and language are important in facilitating reflective learning. Facilitators should be aware of how they speak to a group. For example, they should be aware of how fast they talk, the tone of voice they use, and how loudly or softly they speak. Cultural sensitivity is important again, as well as the intentional use of voice in facilitation. The specific language that is used is important as well. The facilitator should use age and culture appropriate language, make sure that his/her speech is clear, and that the style of speech is positive and supportive. Other important techniques include the knowledge and use of individual's names within the group and the use of both silence and humor. In addition to using active listening skills, the facilitator solicits information from group members by asking questions and rephrasing responses. Open-ended questions are used to bring out thoughts and ideas from group members. Questions such as "What did you notice about how you worked together?" elicit more thoughtful responses than "Did you work together?"

As part of the verbal guiding, the facilitator asks a series of effective questions that encourage participants to share observations and personal meanings. The sequence of questioning moves from concrete levels dealing with descriptions of what happened to abstract levels dealing with analysis and evaluation of what happened. Two models exist to aid facilitators in developing the sequence of concrete and abstract questions. Priest and Naismith (1993) developed the funneling approach that is seen in Figure 4. The review questions are based on reviewing or replaying the experience to make sure that everyone has an overall view of what happened. The recall and remember questions identify more specific incidents within the total experience. The affect and effect questions are designed to elicit the impact caused by the incidents raised from the previous questions. At this point, individuals share feelings and talk about emotions. The summation questions help participants understand the learning they have gained from the experience. When participants are able to identify new learning, they can then apply it to other situations. The application questions help participants identify where they might use the learning, thus reinforcing it. The last questions, the commitment questions, ask individuals for a plan of action to put the new learning into place.

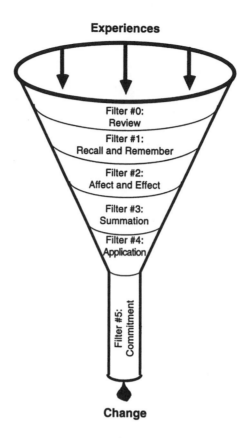

Figure 4: The debriefing funnel.

Reprinted by permission from Simon Priest and Michael A. Gass, 1997, *Effective Leadership in Adventure Planning*, (Champaign, IL: Human Kinetics).

TABLE 1: Cognitive Hierarchy

Cognitive Thought	Debriefing Function	Corresponding Questions
Concrete Levels		
Knowledge (memory)	Review and describe	What did you do when . . .?
Comprehension (understand)	events, feelings, thoughts, and problems.	What happened when . . ? How did you feel when . . .?
Application (usage)		What did your group do when . . .?
Abstract Levels		
Analysis (relationships)	Make comparisons.	What was the highlight for you?
Synthesis (creative)	Relate to daily life.	What was the most challenging?
Evaluation (opinion)	Propose solutions. Examine values.	Does this remind you of anything? What have you learned today that may help you in the future? What have you learned about you?

From Hammel (1986).

The second model, developed by Quinsland and Van Ginkel (1984), begins at the concrete level with questions pertaining to knowledge (remembering information), comprehension (interpreting or explaining information), and application (using information). The model then proceeds to abstract levels with questions pertaining to analysis (detecting relationships between separate pieces of information), synthesis (putting information together in new and creative ways), and evaluation (making judgments about the value of information.

Conclusion

Being a facilitator can sometimes seem complex and overwhelming. The skills require practice and feedback. What follows in this chapter is a method for giving and receiving feedback on facilitation of reflective learning activities. It is set up in a format that can be copied and taken into the field and is meant to be a quick quantitative assessment. The form is not meant to be a stand-alone tool, but meant to serve as a method to develop dialog between facilitator and observer about techniques that the facilitator did well, and suggestions for improvement. The form includes the broad areas of "Physical Set-up," "Personal Safety," "Non-verbal Communication of Facilitator," and "Verbal Communication of Facilitator." Within each broad category are listed specific categories, and within those, specific actions or behaviors to be observed. The rating scale ranges from poor to excellent, with five choices in between. Space at the end of the assessment tool is provided for qualitative comments.

Reflective Learning Facilitator Feedback

Activity Set-Up
Location

- appropriate for goals   poor 1 2 3 4 5 excellent
- accessibility   poor 1 2 3 4 5 excellent
- outside distractions   poor 1 2 3 4 5 excellent
- environmental hazards   poor 1 2 3 4 5 excellent

Physical Set-Up

- inclusive shape   poor 1 2 3 4 5 excellent
- level of participants   poor 1 2 3 4 5 excellent
- location of distractions, sun, etc.   poor 1 2 3 4 5 excellent

Equipment/Materials

- appropriate for activity   poor 1 2 3 4 5 excellent
- in good working order   poor 1 2 3 4 5 excellent
- facilitator knows how to use materials   poor 1 2 3 4 5 excellent

Techniques

- appropriate sequencing   poor 1 2 3 4 5 excellent
- clear directions   poor 1 2 3 4 5 excellent
- appropriate structure provided   poor 1 2 3 4 5 excellent
- flexibility   poor 1 2 3 4 5 excellent
- appropriate time management   poor 1 2 3 4 5 excellent

Personal Safety
Physical Safety

- boundaries of natural environment set   poor 1 2 3 4 5 excellent
- participants prepared for conditions   poor 1 2 3 4 5 excellent
- appropriate safety equipment available   poor 1 2 3 4 5 excellent
- accident response protocol in place   poor 1 2 3 4 5 excellent
- appropriate touching   poor 1 2 3 4 5 excellent
- awareness of body clock issues   poor 1 2 3 4 5 excellent

Emotional Safety

- ground rules set and adhered to   poor 1 2 3 4 5 excellent
- self disclosure modeled   poor 1 2 3 4 5 excellent
- proper "level" of disclosure monitored   poor 1 2 3 4 5 excellent
- use of Full Value Contract   poor 1 2 3 4 5 excellent
- valuing of individual differences   poor 1 2 3 4 5 excellent

Nonverbal Communication
Presence

- competence/confidence   poor   1   2   3   4   5   excellent
- humility   poor   1   2   3   4   5   excellent
- approachability   poor   1   2   3   4   5   excellent
- caring presence   poor   1   2   3   4   5   excellent

Physical Position Within Group

- positioning (where located in group)   poor   1   2   3   4   5   excellent
- same level as participants   poor   1   2   3   4   5   excellent
- cultural sensitivity   poor   1   2   3   4   5   excellent

Physical Attributes

- body posture   poor   1   2   3   4   5   excellent
- facial expressions   poor   1   2   3   4   5   excellent
- eye contact   poor   1   2   3   4   5   excellent
- hand/body movements   poor   1   2   3   4   5   excellent
- cultural sensitivity   poor   1   2   3   4   5   excellent

Verbal Communication
Voice

- cadence (wpm)   poor   1   2   3   4   5   excellent
- tone/inflection   poor   1   2   3   4   5   excellent
- volume   poor   1   2   3   4   5   excellent

Language

- age and culture appropriate language   poor   1   2   3   4   5   excellent
- clarity   poor   1   2   3   4   5   excellent
- style (positive, supportive, etc.)   poor   1   2   3   4   5   excellent

Techniques

- knowledge and use of names   poor   1   2   3   4   5   excellent
- use of open-ended questions   poor   1   2   3   4   5   excellent
- soliciting information   poor   1   2   3   4   5   excellent
- use of silence   poor   1   2   3   4   5   excellent
- use of humor   poor   1   2   3   4   5   excellent

Additional Comments:

3

Ethical Practices of Reflective Learning: Guidelines for Achieving Best Practices and Results

Reflective learning can be a powerful tool for client growth, whether it is in a classroom, corporate boardroom, or therapy room. Regardless of its application, probably one of the most important considerations of its use is the appropriateness of actual practices. For if reflective learning is influential enough to develop effective and beneficial changes, the converse can also be true. When used inappropriately (as with all change processes), reflective learning can lead to miseducational experiences, counterproductive processes and outcomes, or contraindicative treatments. The purpose of this chapter is to provide some general guidelines toward producing appropriate and productive reflective learning practices and avoiding counterproductive ones.

Embodied in achieving best practices in reflective learning are two interrelated concepts: (1) appropriate focus or "depth" of the reflective experience for clients and (2) appropriate ethical decision making processes in reflective learning. For facilitators using reflective learning techniques, paying attention to these two areas is one way to increase the likelihood that both the goals as well as the methods of reaching clients' objectives are done in an appropriate manner.

Maintaining Appropriate Focus and Depth of Clients' Experiences

As portrayed through this book, client needs and program purposes can vary a great deal when using reflective learning theories and practices. Client type, client objectives, difference between group, and individual goals all contribute to this variation facilitators need to monitor and address with clients. One additional factor that is critical to handle is the ability of facilitators to monitor appropriate psychological depth of reflective learning experiences.

The idea of psychological depth refers to the concept that reflective learning experiences, while targeted to address certain client objectives, often evoke powerful associations with clients. When these associations match appropriate objectives, the learning and applications from these connections serve as the basis for functional client growth. However, when these associations don't match, when associations are made at a different "level" than intended, the interaction between client objectives and learning associations need to be "recalibrated" in a manner that works best for the client.

In an effort to address this dynamic, Gillis et al. (1991) outlined four basic mediums where reflective learning techniques are used. These categories included recreation, education, training/development, and therapeutic focuses. Adapted from Ringer and Gillis (1995), the primary goals of each of these mediums and their distinguishing features are seen in Table 2 .

From this Table, it can be seen that the goals and distinguishing features of reflective learning experiences vary with programming intent. One of the difficulties that one can imagine, based on this

TABLE 2: Primary goals and distinguishing features of various levels of reflective learning experiences.

	Recreation	Education	Training/ Development	Therapeutic
Primary goal	Fun, laughter challenge, excitement initiative, etc.	Change in sense of identity or self-concept	Learning associated with a generic theme such as cooperation, communication, and trust	Learning about interpersonal processes that will be applied with participant's significant others
Distinguishing features	The primary focus is on enjoyment or life enrichment	Often associated with learning for an occupation, vocation, or course of study	Associated with the desire to improve behavior in important relationships. Often work related.	Often (but not always) applied to remedy personal dysfunction. Usually preceded by client assessment.

information, is when clients find themselves at a different focus than the sponsoring program. For example, say that in a reflective learning experience designed for educational purposes, a client starts to recall a situation that deeply affected him/her at a more therapeutic level. In such a situation, facilitators need to be prepared to appropriately guide the individual to the intended programming level and agreed purposes of the group during the reflective learning experience.

How does a facilitator handle situations where clients find themselves at the wrong level? One first place to start is with the concept of "agreed purposes." The concept of agreed purposes refers to the idea that the facilitator, umbrella organization, and group participants have proactively and jointly established a shared purpose for the learning experience based on the past history and future applications/needs of the group (Ringer & Gillis, 1995). These purposes should be initially, repeatedly, and openly shared with group members so they may serve as a "grounding" focus for groups as they progress through reflective learning experiences. Such efforts serve as a positive proactive approach to insure clients are receiving the type of experience they are seeking.

Despite the planning involved behind the concept of "agreed purposes," there will be times where participants will find themselves at the wrong level of programming. When a client finds him/herself at a "lighter" level of programming than intended (e.g., a recreational focus instead of a training/development focus), facilitators appropriately bring the group back into focus by reminding them of the agreed upon task at hand.

Handling situations where clients find themselves at a "deeper" level of programming generally takes more intentional work to align with intended objectives. As stated by Ringer and Gillis (1995), several problems may occur in moving back to the agreed-upon level of the group. "First, the leader's empathetic response may lead a participant or the whole group into further discussion at the deeper level. Second, the leader ... (inappropriately) "cuts off" the participant for fear of deepening the level in the whole group." (p. 48).

One way to handle such a situation is to appropriately guide the client to the context of the specific situation that they are in right at this moment with these group members. This would include focusing the individual on what he or she is saying with this group at this particular time. An example of a question to ask is "how does disclosing this information at this time make sense to discuss with this group given the objective of the learning experience?" For greater assistance with issues such as these, readers are referred to Ringer and Gillis (1995).

Ethical Practices in Reflective Learning

Other guidelines and practices exist to assist facilitators in the use of "best practices" with reflective learning. These are often referred to as ethical practices. Ethical practices can generally be defined as practices that are "morally right" or those that are in the best interests of the client. Ethical practices not only address outcomes (i.e., the "ends") but also the processes by which those outcomes are achieved (i.e., the "means").

While there are many more advanced and sophisticated discussions on ethical practices than offered here, the following are a series of seven guidelines from Priest and Gass (1997a) that tend to support ethical decision making with reflective learning.[1] Specifically, the seven guidelines relate to competence, integrity, responsibility, respect, concern, recognition, and objectivity. Although developed for other forms of experiential practices, these seven guidelines are offered for professionals using reflective learning practices.

Be aware that following such guidelines does not release you from the need to apply ethical judgment. Ethical guidelines like the ones presented here have limitations. Such guidelines may conflict with the framework of certain cultures, requiring you to adapt them in such instances. Or, you may find yourself in a situation in which a conflict exists among legal, organizational, and ethical

---

[1] Probably one of the brightest developments of ethical decision making for outdoor leadership is the formulation of ethical guidelines by the Association of Experiential Education's Therapeutic Adventure Professional Group (AEE, 1992). You can find another version of these guidelines in the ethics section of the program accreditation standards identified in the Manual of Program Accreditation Standards for Adventure Programs (Williamson & Gass, 1993). These guidelines were created with the support of the American Psychological Association (APA), the American Alliance of Marriage and Family Therapists (AAMFT), Council on Outdoor Education for the American Alliance of Health, Physical Education, & Dance (COE/AAHPERD), Council of Accreditation of Services for Families and Children (CASFC), and the Worldwide Outfitters and Guides Association (WOGA).

guidelines. Conflict between ethical guidelines and their interpretation will likely arise and lead to dilemmas for you to resolve as best you can. No matter what the course of action you select, the summum bonum (i.e., do no harm) ethic you as a professional follow to resolve dilemmas should be guided by empathy for clients.

Competence

Conduct experiences only at your level of competence. Provide services within the boundaries of your education, training, supervision, experience, and practice. Take reasonable steps to ensure the competence of your work. Avoid situations in which personal problems or conflicts will impair your performance or judgment. Stay abreast of current information in the field. Participate in ongoing professional efforts to maintain your knowledge, practice, and skills.

Integrity

Conduct experiences with integrity—meaning with focus on honesty, fairness, and with respect to the interactions between both clients and peers. Avoid false, misleading, or deceptive statements when describing or reporting qualifications, services, products, or fees. Be aware of how your personal belief system, values, needs, and limitations affect clients.

Responsibility

Conduct experiences with responsibility by upholding the ethical principles of your work. Be clear with clients as to what everyone's roles and obligations are. Accept responsibility for your behavior and decisions. Adapt methods to the needs of different populations. Ensure that you possess an adequate basis for professional judgments. Do not offer services when the constraints of limited contact will not benefit client needs (e.g., promising a single day reflective learning experience will resolve a deep issue for a therapeutic or corporate population). Continue services only so long as it is reasonably clear that clients will benefit.

Respect

Conduct experiences with respect for the rights and dignity of clients. Respect the fundamental rights, dignity, and worth of all people. Respect clients' rights to privacy, confidentiality, and self-determination within the limits of the law. Strive to be sensitive to cultural and individual differences, including those due to age, gender, race, ethnicity, national origin, religion, sexual orientation, disability, and socioeconomic status. Do not engage in sexual or other harassment or exploitation of clients. Respect clients' rights to make decisions as well as help them understand the consequences of their choices. Provide clients with appropriate information about the nature of services and their rights, risks, and responsibilities. Offer an opportunity to discuss the results, interpretations, and conclusions of the reflective learning experience with clients. Respect clients' rights to refuse consent to services and activities. Obtain informed consent from clients and, when appropriate, their parents or guardians before beginning services. Accurately represent your competence, training, education, and experience relevant to the program you are delivering.

Concern

Conduct experiences with concern for the well being of clients, being sensitive to client needs and well being. Provide for the appropriate physical needs of clients. Monitor the appropriate use of emotional risk in reflective learning experiences. Assist in obtaining other services if the program cannot for appropriate reasons provide the professional help clients may need. Plan experiences with the clients' best interests in mind both during and after the program. Respect clients' rights to decide the extent to which confidential material can be made public, except under extreme conditions as required by law to prevent a clear and immediate danger to a person or persons.

Recognition

Conduct experiences with recognition of your focus on social responsibility and social justice. Be aware of your responsibilities to community and society. Appropriately encourage the development of standards and policies that serve your clients' interests as well as those of the public. Respect the property of others.

Objectivity

Conduct experiences with objectivity by avoiding dual relationships with clients that impair professional judgment. Do not exploit or mislead clients or other leaders during and after professional relationships. This includes, but is not limited to, business relationships, close personal friendships, family relationships, sexual relations, and otherwise inappropriate physical contact.

Reflection Activities

Pre-Experience and Combinations
(Pre/Post-Experience)

Frontloading

Description: This is a "proactive" reflective technique that is useful when one learning experience follows another. It is a great way to help create intentional focuses on participants' learning experiences. It also helps to increase learner responsibility and center thinking around how to extract intentional learning from experiences.

Population: Children through adults. The language of the questions should be adapted to the age of the participants.

Group Size: 1-15. The ideal group size is 8-15 participants; it gets a bit long after 15 people.

Time: Dependent on the number of people, but plan for about 5-15 minutes.

Activity Level: Low.

Goals

- To utilize elements of previous learning experiences to enrich learning.
- To "pre-identify" focused areas of learning prior to beginning experiences.
- To heighten the group awareness around potential learning.

Materials: None needed. Writing down identified areas of focus and group commitments can be helpful, but is not necessary.

Procedure: Following a learning experience and before beginning another related experience, ask the group to consider one or more of the following questions:

- What do you think this next learning experience might teach you?
- Why do you think this learning might be important?
- What do you recall from past learning that you wanted to work on in situations like this?

After asking these questions, give the group approximately 30-60 seconds to think of individual responses. After that time, invite people to share their responses with the group. Inform the group that responses are not to be debated, but questions of clarification are encouraged. Ask people to make a mental note of what their individual and group responses were, and let them know that you will be asking about this information once the experience is completed. After the group completes the experience, center some of the reflective process on comparing this information to what occurred with their learning.

Thoughts: In essence, with frontloading you focus clients' attention on certain distinct learning outcomes that you have ascertained as valuable. By doing this, you direct the reflection after the experience and reemphasize the learning. Priest & Gass (1997a) have classified frontloading questions into categories, some of which include:

- Revisiting questions: "What behaviors or performances were promised and learned from the last activity?"
- Objectives questions: "What are the aims of the activity and what do you think might be learned or gained from this experience?"
- Motivational questions: "Why might this experience be important and how might it relate to your life?"
- Functional questions: "What type of behaviors do you think will help bring about success and how might you make optimal use of these?
- Dysfunctional questions: "What type of behaviors do you think will hinder your success and how might you overcome these barriers?

Participant assessment is obviously critical in deciding on appropriate areas for frontloading and questions that will empower individuals. When done appropriately, this type of approach can create more meaningful and longer lasting learning.

Give a Little, Get a Lot

Description: This activity helps group members focus on the qualities that they as individuals bring to the group and what qualities they receive from being a group member.

Population: Adolescents through adults.

Group Size: Anywhere from 3-20 people. Dynamics of the experience will vary with changing group sizes.

Time: Dependent on the number of people, but plan for 10 minutes organizational time plus 2 minutes per person in the group.

Activity Level: Low.

Goals

- To have individuals consider how each group member is a part of the group.
- To have individuals consider how being a member of the group is a benefit to each person.
- To celebrate being members of a group.

Materials

- One water bottle per person.
- Water or some appropriate drinkable liquid.
- One extra water bottle with a cap (a water bottle larger than the others works well, but is not necessary).

Procedure: Prior to beginning the experience, have each group member fill his or her water bottle with fresh, clean water (or other appropriate drinkable liquid) and join the group in a circle. Have participants sit in a comfortable position where they can see and hear everyone.

When everyone is comfortable, ask group members to consider a quality they bring to the group that benefits the group. Ask them to think about this in silence, and encourage them to take a minimum of 1-2 minutes in thinking about a response that they would be willing to publicly share with the group.

After one to two minutes of reflection, ask group members to place their full water bottles in front of them. Ask for a volunteer to go first. This person should take the full water bottle and pour a small amount of water from it into the empty water bottle. As the water is being poured, the individual states the personal quality he or she contributes to the group. Then the individual passes the empty water bottle to the person next in the circle and the procedure is repeated. The bottle is passed around the circle until everyone has contributed a small portion of water from personal water bottles into the "group" water bottle. If the bottle is passed to a person who is not quite ready to respond, he or she can "pass," for the time being and have the opportunity to contribute as the bottle comes around again.

Once everyone has completed the task, take the group water bottle, place a cover on it and shake it up. Then ask group members to think about what qualities they have received as a result of being a member of the group. Once they have had appropriate reflection time, have one group member volunteer to begin pouring water from the group bottle into his or her personal water bottle, stating the quality received from the group.

In one sense, they are replacing what they have given to the group. They are not getting back the same qualities they gave, but are receiving a distillation of what the group has produced. After everyone has completed the task, ask the group to celebrate what has occurred by taking part in a "ceremonial toast" to the group success.

A final consideration is to ask people to compare what they gave to the group and what they received—was it worth the "cost" or "risk?" What were factors that made it so?

Thoughts: As a nice framework to the activity, ask people to consider the value of water and share their thoughts to the group. Answers provided by group members (e.g., source of life, basis for all things, source of refreshment/revitalization, necessary for life) often mirror responses the group may share in the activity and serve to nurture the creative process.

Instead of passing the bottle around the circle, the facilitator can place it in the middle of the group circle. Announce that when people are ready, one at a time they can step forward and pour a small portion of water from their personal water bottle into the empty water bottle. While doing this, they should state the quality they bring to the group. Some advantages of this variation are that: (1) people can go when they are ready and "physically step up" to bring something to the group; and (2) people can make their presentation when they are ready and don't have to worry about the "pass" option. A possible disadvantage is that it is harder to hear and visually see people making this presentation as they move to the circle (e.g., their back will be toward some of the group when they pour in their water).

This activity can be divided into two sections. At the beginning of one day people can contribute from their water bottles to the group bottle what they add to the group, and then at the end of the day they can state what they received from the group. Placing the water in a refreshing spot (e.g., refrigerator, tied down in a cold mountain stream) for retrieval at the end of the day is a good consideration.

As the group water bottle fills up, people must take into account that space must be provided for each group member. A facilitator can offer this as a "caution" in the beginning of the exercise, or allow potential "teachable moments" to spill out!

Goals Pyramid

Description: The group builds a posterboard pyramid based on their goals for an experience. The activity is divided into three parts: beginning goals, secondary goals that are built on the primary goals, and feedback on the accomplishment of both goals. This activity is best used in an experience that has a long-term format, such as a course or a long trip.

Population: Children through adults.

Group Size: Between 15 and 20.

Time: One hour for each of the three parts of the activity.

Goals

- To give students an opportunity to verbalize their goals for an experience.
- To be able to build on the first goals stated with additional goals.
- To give students feedback on their goals.

Materials

- Poster board
- Markers
- Transparent tape
- Laminating paper

Activity Level: Low.

Procedure: Make a large triangle out of the poster board. Divide the triangle into thirds. The first third represents the first part of the experience, the second third represents the second part of the experience and the third represents each individual's "personal power piece." You will need to make as many top pieces as the number of people you have in the group. For example if you have ten people in the group, you will have one bottom piece, one middle piece, and 10 top pieces.

Cut the bottom part of the triangle into puzzle pieces. Make as many pieces as you have group members. NOTE: make a drawing of the section with the puzzle pieces before you cut the pieces out so that you have a template to go back to if the group has trouble solving the puzzle. Also, somehow mark the side of the puzzle that faces up, either by getting poster paper that has a different color on each side, or by physically marking each piece with a dot. My puzzle pieces are very angular, not like real puzzle pieces. I have found that simple works best.

At the beginning of the experience, set aside time for group members to think of an important goal they have for the experience. Have each person pick a puzzle piece and write their goal on the top side of the piece.

Direct each person to share the goal with the rest of the group. When everyone has shared, instruct the group to put the puzzle together. Discussion topics include: how our group is like the puzzle; how we help each other reach our goals; etc.

Tape the puzzle together and if possible laminate it so that it is sturdy and will last.

At some point during the experience (usually half way, or at some natural dividing point), have the group do the same thing with the second part of the triangle. Cut the section into puzzle pieces, have students write a goal for the second half of the experience on a puzzle piece, put the puzzle together, and tape and laminate it to the first part of the triangle. Good discussion topics for this section include accomplishment of the first goals, building new goals from the first goals, etc.

The top piece (the "personal power piece") is used at the final stage of the group experience. Each person receives his or her own piece to keep. I have conducted this part of the activity two ways:

1. I have written observations on the top piece that I have made about that person and then presented it to them on the last night of the experience, explaining my observations to them.
2. I have also given each person a blank top piece on the last night, had them draw a small picture that represented themselves during the experience, then passed the pieces around the group and had everyone write a word or two about the person. The piece returns to the original owner with many words of feedback from the entire group.

Thoughts: I have used this activity most successfully in courses that have definite breaks or sections such as a backpacking skills course that included two separate trips and a challenge course management class that included separate sections on low and high elements. Laminating the sections allowed us to take the pyramid to class in order to remind ourselves of our goals. I have also hung the finished pyramid (minus the "personal power pieces") outside my office. Students in the course like being able to explain to other students what the pyramid is and how it worked for them.

Hopes/Fears in a Hat

Description: This activity gives participants an anonymous way to express their hopes and fears for an experience. The activity is usually done at the beginning of an experience, then revisited after the experience is over, to recheck the hopes and fears.

Population: Children through adults.

Group Size: 10-20.

Time: 30 to 60 minutes, depending on the group size and the number of responses.

Activity Level: Low.

Goals

- To provide a way for group members to identify their hopes and fears for an experience.
- To provide a means for individuals to express feelings they may be afraid to share with the group.
- To provide a way for individuals to see if their hopes were realized and if their fears were changed during the experience.

Materials

- 3X5 note cards—enough for at least 4 per person in the group.
- Marking pens.
- One hat or something to put the note cards in.

Procedure: Pass out 4 note cards to each person in the group. Ask them to think about the experience ahead and picture in their minds what they are excited about, or what they hope will happen, and what they are nervous about, or what they fear about the experience. Have them write 2 hopes and 2 fears on their note cards, one per card. Make sure they do not put their names on the cards. Ask them to fold the cards in half and place them in the hat.

Mix up the cards, then pass them around the circle, each person taking one card at a time until all the cards are taken. Have one person start by reading what is on one of his or her cards. Then as a group, discuss what was on the card. Talk openly about people's hopes and fears, so that group members begin to understand that their feelings are similar to other's in the group. Continue this process until all the cards are read.

During the experience, place the cards in a spot that is visible to group members, such as tacked to a wall. When the experience is completed, return to the cards and revisit what was written on them. Were the hopes realized? What happened during the experience to help the hopes become reality? Did the fears change during the experience? What happened that changed the fears?

Thoughts: The cards can also be revisited at various points during the experience and used as a way to guide the group. "Are our hopes being realized? What do we need to do to make sure they are realized? What about our fears? Are they still present? How can we change them?"

Journals

Description: Journals are a written method for participants to record information, reactions to experiences, and personal learning.

Population: Children through adults. The journal mode and language should be adapted to the age of the participants.

Group Size: Unlimited.

Time: Dependent on the goals of the journal.

Activity Level: Low.

Goals

- To utilize a written mode of reflection.
- To allow participants an opportunity to record information, observations, reactions, and personal learning.

Materials: Journals can be formal with actual notebooks used, or can be more informal using loose pieces of paper, depending on the goals of the exercise.

Procedure: Depending on the specific goals of the journal exercise, several modes of journals are available to facilitators.

Log Journals: A written record of facts such as activities accomplished, who took what role in the activities, the weather, etc. This type of writing stimulates an awareness of what happened in an experience. The writing itself can be used as a record of events in an experience, which is an important part of the reflection process. In the process of writing the log, other insights about the experience may come to light and be written down. The specific facts in the journal may also be used later in the experience as a tool for reflection. The facilitator may ask participants to read back through their journals and pick out a particular instance that was important for them. Used in this way, the journals are an aid to help participants remember what happened to them, and as a jumping off point for further discussion and insight.

Free Response Journals: A form of writing where individuals write continuously for a specific amount of time without being concerned about spelling, grammar, complete sentences, etc. The emphasis is on the generation of writing, and with it, ideas. Students are typically instructed to focus on writing nonstop for short periods of time. (Rossiter, 1999, pg. 28). The end result is the compilation of ideas, thoughts and insights into an experience. It is a safe place where individuals can experiment with the process of writing and focus on getting out their ideas rather than focusing on their writing skills. In order to help participants become comfortable with this writing style, facilitators should give as little structure as possible. Instructions such as "write about your day" allow freedom of expression, yet give some structure to the exercise. As participants become familiar and comfortable with the free writing process, "focused free writing" can be introduced which provides more specific topics around which participants focus their writing. Focused topics might include looking at leadership during an experience, or interactions of group members. The focused topics provide more structure, still allowing for free response and generation of ideas.

Critical Incident Journals: A method to stimulate critical thinking, and extract meaning from events. The purpose of this journal mode is to give students the opportunity to record and reflect on specific experiences. Participants are instructed to focus on, write about, and extract meaning from specific significant events that happened during an experience. An example is a "judgement journal" (Priest, 1988) in which students analyze decisions made during the day, looking at how judgement was involved, and what learning can be taken from the process. Participants are given structure as to what to focus their writing on, and expected to process the experience, verbalize what was important about the experience, and describe what learning they are taking from the experience. This type of journal solidifies the process of reflection by helping individuals extract meaning from experiences.

Dialectic (Double Entry) Journals: A method used to critically evaluate information by writing down facts, observations, notes, etc., and later reacting to the original writing. The double entry journal is set up using two pages facing each other or one page that is divided in half vertically with a line drawn down the center. On the left side of the page (or the left-hand page), individuals write down information obtained during an experience, through reading, through a teaching session, etc. The entries are similar to what was done in the log journal: observations, notes, summaries, etc. On the right side of the page (or the right hand page), reactions to the original entries are made. This gives the individual a chance to reflect on the observations made and record reactions and synthesize knowledge. The left-hand side is done first, as close to the actual experience as possible. The reactions are completed at a later time, giving the individual a chance to digest and reflect on the experience.

Prompt Journals: a directive mode of journals with participants responding to questions posed by the facilitator. Depending on the goals of the facilitator, a variety of questions could be asked such as:

- questions pertaining to observations made during an experience (What did you notice about the techniques used to accomplish the Wall?)
- questions that ask the individual to think about the importance of an event (What was important for you about the climbing session today? Why was it important?)
- questions that ask participants to extract meaning from experiences (What did you learn about yourself this past week?)
- questions asking for future thinking (How will you use what you learned at home with your family?)

It is important that the questions are open-ended, with the individual being able to write extensively about the topic. Questions should also be pertinent to the population and hold their interest.

Group Journals: A shared book in which participants take turns recording events and impressions, entering their thoughts, and commenting on previous entries or group discussions. This type of journal tends to foster group cohesion and creativity, as participants are able to read the entries of others and add their own thoughts. If the facilitator is involved in the process, it gives him or her the opportunity to read what participants are thinking about and how they view their experiences. Issues can be brought to the attention of the whole group, or used as topics for discussion during reflection times. Individuals may ask questions of the group, and responses written in the group journal. This journal can also be used as a closure activity. Individual copies can be given out to participants at the end of the experience, giving each person a written record of the group's thoughts and ideas.

Project Journals: Regular entries related to a future project to be accomplished by an individual or by the entire group. This type of journal is useful for long-term experiences and offers participants the opportunity to reflect on the process of working on a project. For example, if a group was planning a service day and was involved in the planning, preparation, and logistics of the day, a project journal would be a place where participants could record the process of planning, their reactions to events, people, etc., and reflections on the process and the learning. A variation on the project journal is the goal journal, in which participants write about the process they go through to reach a stated goal. An example would be a student whose goal is to speak up more in the group, would write about how he or she worked on the goal that day, what it felt like to work on it, plans for continuing working on it, etc.

Thoughts: Journals provide an avenue for reflection that is different from verbally speaking. Some individuals who are reluctant to speak up in a group find that journals provide a welcome place to express what is on their minds. Journals help open up the thought process for some individuals, who are later able to speak about their writing. The possibilities for creativity in journals are endless, with the use of artwork, poetry, stories, readings, etc. Journals are a wonderful medium for expression.

Partner Reflection

Description: This reflection technique highlights the advantages associated with constructing dyad (and sometimes triad) partnerships to heighten client perspectives and learning. It can be done proactively prior to the learning experience, or afterward as a form of debriefing. When done correctly, it can instill a synergistic and reflective series of positive interactions with the group.

Population: Children through adults.

Group Size: Two and higher. It actually is a wonderful technique to use when facilitators find themselves in situations where group sizes would make small group discussions difficult (e.g., groups larger than 15).

Time: 20 to 40 minutes.

Activity Level: Low.

Goals

- To provide a vehicle for group members to share feedback on one another's behaviors.
- To offer an "external" reflection of another person's interactions.
- To instill a sense of careful observation of another person.
- To provide a structured opportunity to give one-on-one feedback to another person.

Materials: In the reflective exercise described below, writing implements, small pieces of paper, and a hat or similar type of container.

Procedure: (The procedure described here is one variation—others are listed later). Before beginning the learning experience, the facilitator asks the group to take a pen and small piece of paper and write their name on the paper. After this is completed, group members place the slip of paper into the hat. After mixing up the pieces of paper, each person draws a name out of the hat (other than their own name) and keeps that person's name to himself or herself. If the person draws out their own name, they place it back in the hat and draw out another name.

After everyone has a name, the facilitator announces that besides participating in the experience and observing the whole group's interaction, they are to especially watch this person's behavior and efforts during the learning experience. In many ways, it is akin to having observers watch with "their antennas up," identifying:

- behaviors of this person that seem to contribute to their own and the group's successes;
- what happened in the group that allowed this person with the opportunities take full advantage of their efforts;
- when the person was most likely to be successful with their learning (e.g., Kiser, Piercy, & Lipchik, 1993, p. 236).

In the group reflection time, each person is asked to share with the group their observations of their partner.

Thoughts: Sometimes having observers identified ahead of time makes people feel more comfortable, but this also can change people's interactions during the learning experience (which may be beneficial!). People can also "partner up" and observe one another. Following the learning experience, yet prior to the group reflection time, dyads can be given the opportunity to dialogue about their observations of one another. In the full group, edited versions of this dialogue can be shared as a part of the group reflection experience and shared with others' observations.

Planting Seeds for the Car Ride Home

Description: This is a "proactive" reflective technique used at the beginning of learning experiences to help create a positive focus on participants' experiences. Not only have I found it a great way to "double check" some of the hypotheses and thoughts I have about working with a group as a facilitator, it also centers the group's thinking around how to create a beneficial experience.

Population: Children through adults. The language of the questions should be adapted to the age of the participants. The language presented here represents an adult corporate group.

Group Size: 1-25. The ideal size is about 8-12 participants; it gets a bit long after 25 people.

Time: Dependent on the number of people, but plan for about 10 minutes organizational time plus 5 minutes per person in the group.

Activity Level: Low.

Goals

- To learn group members' names.
- To have each person identify a particular valued behavior.
- To have the group members identify what they view as success.
- To plant "seeds" of success into the group's value system.
- To enhance the facilitator's group assessment.

Materials

- Flip chart with multi-colored magic markers.
- Writing boards are also fine, just make sure you have enough room to write everyone's responses.

Procedure: At the beginning of a session, ask people to gather around in a circle. Ask them to identify three pieces of information to share with the group and tell them that you will write down their answers on the flip chart. These pieces of information are:

1. their name (how/what they would like to be called for your time together);
2. their count-on behavior;
3. their car ride conversation home.

The last two pieces obviously need explanation, and here's a sample "script" of what you might say:

Count-on behavior: For your "count-on" behavior I would like you to describe to the group a behavior that you can generally be counted on to provide. This could be your "trademark" of sorts in your organization, group, or school. It is something that you can always be counted on to provide to the group, particularly when they need it. For example, if we enter a learning experience today that group members find particularly challenging, they would turn to you for this "count-on behavior" that would help the group in some way. Group members know that they can turn to you as a "resource" of sorts and you will provide "lots" of it. Your "count-on behavior" may be something that is obvious to the present group members, or it may be something you provide to the group without anyone ever realizing it.

Car ride conversation: After your experience here today, someone is going to ask you the proverbial question, "What did you think of that experience you did today?" There's no getting around it—whether it is your spouse, colleague, or trusted friend—you're going to get asked this question.

Let's say it is on the car ride home from our work together. A trusted friend turns to you and asks "What did you think of what we did today?" You respond truthfully (and not because I'm in the back seat of the car making you respond this way), "It actually was excellent—I learned more than I thought I would. I was engaged in the process and I really see how this will make a difference in our workplace."

What I am interested in is what would have to happen today in order for you to answer in such a way? What would we be doing? How would we be accomplishing it? What was happening to make this occur? I'm also interested in how I, a person who doesn't know you as well as you know yourself, would recognize this happening. What would be going on in order for such a "car ride" conversation to occur?

After group members have thought about the three pieces of information, have them go around the circle and describe each piece. Either write the information down on the flip chart, or have them write it down.

Thoughts: I have found starting learning experiences in this manner to be very beneficial for my assessment of group members. Not only do I learn their names, I observe how they interact and treat one another.

Finding out what people "claim" as their count-on behaviors can also be enlightening. Group members can often learn a great deal about how people view themselves and how this relates to experiential learning exercises later on in trainings.

"Car ride conversation" predictions are rich from a number of perspectives. One is that they inform others (including the facilitator!) what participants want to have happen during the learning experience. Second, they create an expectation in the group of working toward these types of behaviors. Third, they direct individuals to a "framed expectation" that the learning experience is about being successful. This creates a wonderful reciprocal learning loop between individuals, fellow participants, and facilitators that if fostered correctly will result in such experiences. Unfortunately, many participants enter learning experiences expecting the worst. Engaging participants in describing methods and areas that they are interested in is one of the first critical learning steps toward establishing effective learning mediums.

Reflection Activities

**Post-Experience
(No Props Involved)**

Finish the Story

Description: A fun activity that allows the participants to summarize some of the activities they have experienced.

Population: Children through adults.

Group Size: Under 25.

Time: Variable depending on program goals.

Activity Level: Low.

Goals

To help participants create a shared story about their experience.

Materials: None.

Procedure: Ask the participants to sit in a circle. Explain that they are going to create a story that captures memorable moments they had while participating in the experience. The trick is that each person can only add one word at a time to the story. Go around the circle and have each person say one word based on what was said by the person ahead of him or her. For example the first 5 participants might begin the story as follows: Participant 1 "We"; Participant 2 "have"; Participant 3 "become"; Participant 4 "friends"; Participant 5 "today." All the remaining group members continue adding words. When members of the group have had a chance to go around the circle at least twice, the story should be finished.

Thoughts: The facilitator should be writing down the words as participants speak them. This can be a fun and relaxed ending activity that can be allowed to go on for many minutes. Another variation is to ask participants to take the story that has been constructed and create a song with these words as the lyrics.

Human Machine

Description: This exercise is a creative way for participants to metaphorically relate their experience to a particular part of a machine.

Population: Children through adults.

Time: Fifteen minutes, depending on the size of the group.

Activity Level: Low.

Goals

- To give participants the opportunity to make metaphorical connections between their experiences and a machine.
- To have participants share their experiences and feelings about an activity.

Materials: None.

Procedure: Have the group sit in a circle. Explain that you want the group to think of themselves as a car (or other well-known piece of machinery) in the previous experience. Then explain that you want each person to think about what piece of the car he or she was during the experience. Was she the horn? Was he the engine? Was she a flat tire?

After the group has had a few minutes to think, ask someone to start by explaining what part of the car he or she was, and why that part was chosen. After the explanation is finished, have that person enter the middle of the circle and act out what part of the car he or she chose. You may want that person to stay in the center of the circle, and as each successive person speaks, he or she enters the circle and adds to the car.

Thoughts: Be sure to choose a well-known piece of machinery so that everyone is comfortable with identifying particular parts. If individuals have difficulty, you may want to brainstorm what parts are in the machinery and what function each part plays.

People Sculpture

Description: In this activity one person physically moves another person into a position that represents some aspect of the experience for them. It is a physical way to express emotion.

Goals

- To have students physically moving during a processing session.
- To allow students to express themselves through movement.
- To give students an opportunity to express emotions felt during an experience.

Materials: None.

Activity Level: Moderate; people are actively moving around.

Procedure: Break students into pairs.

Explain to the group that you want one partner to be an artist who will create a sculpture by moving their partner into a position based on a question posed. Questions can include: what did you notice about yourself in this activity; express how you communicated with others in the group during this activity; express an emotion that you felt during the activity, etc. Questions can be concrete or more abstract.

Partner teams work together to decide who will be the clay and who will be the artist. The artist moves the clay into a position based on the question posed. When everyone is done, each artist explains his or her sculpture. The rest of the group may ask questions to understand the meaning behind the sculpture. The partner teams switch roles and complete the exercise.

Thoughts: This is a fairly simple way to get participants physically involved in expressing themselves about an activity. Make sure that students feel comfortable enough with each other so that moving body parts is acceptable. For some groups, you may want to set guidelines around touching body parts.

A way to run this exercise without involving touching is to give students several colored pipe cleaners and ask them to make a visual representation of a specific question asked. The facilitator may choose colors for individuals, or they may choose the colors themselves.

Scaling or Ranking Experiences

Description: This reflective exercise has been used "internally" by learners since the time self-evaluation and reflection began. What this reflective exercise does is provide "shared evidence" of what people are thinking about the learning. It can be extremely helpful in assessing groups, receiving feedback on the effectiveness of learning, and seeding awareness in a group as to where group members are in their development.

Population: Children through adults. The technique can be adapted for various age levels.

Group Size: 1-30. If the group is larger than 30, have people get into groups with similar scores.

Time: Depends on the level of follow-up to the scaling question. If this is just a quick "check-in," it can be approximately 5-15 seconds in length. Following up the scaling with questions (solution-oriented questions will be used in the description here) can extend this up to 20 or so minutes for a group of 10-12.

Activity Level: Low.

Goals

- To assess the attitudes/opinions/feelings of each group member following a learning experience.
- To assess the effectiveness of a learning experience.
- To heighten the group awareness around each individual's evaluation of the learning experience.

Materials: None.

Procedure: After completing an experience and targeting a specific behavior for reflection, the facilitator asks group members to evaluate how they think they did either personally or as a group (be clear on which one you are looking for) on this behavior. For this description, the behavior targeted will be communication. Participants are asked to use a scale from 0-10, with '0' representing a total lack of communication and '10' being total successful communication. After a brief time (20-30 seconds) to think of their quantitative response, go around the circle to allow each person to share his or her number with the group. This can be done verbally or by holding up the number of fingers that indicates the response.

When sharing responses, the group is able to see the variety in scores. From this, ask participants to share what they did to make their score that particular number and not 1 to 2 points lower. For example, a person may rate their communication as a '5.' You might ask this person to consider those positive elements that "made" the score a '5,' and prevented the score from being lower (e.g., "Nice job—what were the things that you did to make the score a '5' and not a '4' or '3'?"). Focus on building those attributes to increase the evaluative score (e.g., "What small thing could you do as an individual to make your score move from a '5' to a '6'? or "What will you be doing differently as a group when your group is at a '6' or a '7'?").

In this scaling process, the solution-focused approach assists the group and facilitator in gaining a more concrete perception of the problem, but only in light of how it pertains to possible solutions. This approach also emphasizes what participants are doing already that is useful, which directs them to highlight, access, and utilize their strengths.

Thoughts: A "non numerical" version of this can also be used with the thumbs up, sideways, or down technique. Thumbs up means "fully agree", thumbs downwards mean "don't agree at all", and thumbs sideways means "somewhere in between." Using this technique, the solution-oriented question would be around "What did you do so you didn't point your thumb further down?" or "In the next learning experience, if you did something to lead you to raise your thumb, what would you be doing?" This can work well with young children.

Solution oriented processes have proven to be effective with therapeutic (Gass & Gillis, 1995b) and corporate (Priest & Gass, 1997b) groups. Therapeutic examples of scaling can be found in Berg (1994) and Gass & Gillis (1995b).

Set the Record Straight

Description: It is common for individuals who have taken part in an experiential program to feel that some of their behavior as a member of the group might have been misinterpreted by the other group members. This activity allows people to "explain" any behavior they believe might have been misunderstood.

Population: Children through adults.

Group Size: Best for small to medium size groups (maximum 20).

Time: Two minutes per person.

Activity Level: Low.

Goals

- To help participants view their behavior and learn about the connection between the intention of their action and how their behavior might be interpreted by others.

Materials: None.

Procedure: Explain to group participants that sometimes an individual's behavior can be misunderstood when they are a member of a group. Give participants an opportunity to think back on their behavior during the time they were involved in the program. Ask participants to pick one or two times that they feel the group might have misunderstood them. After participants have had a few minutes to think, ask members of the group to "set the record straight" by describing the incident and offering an explanation. Ask each person to offer the final explanation statement about how they would like the group to remember the situation. After each person speaks, ask the group to thank the person who has just spoken.

Thoughts: The leader can ask participants if they are often misunderstood when they demonstrate certain behaviors. Is there a pattern to their misunderstandings? For example when they are in a hurry, frustrated, bored, tired, etc.? Ask participants to think of positive solutions that might help reduce misunderstandings. Finally, ask the participants to think of times they are clearly understood. Are there any patterns? For example when they are in a hurry, frustrated, bored, tired, etc.?

Since the facilitator is part of the group, he or she should model how to respond to each question he/she poses to the group.

Snapshot

Description: This activity helps participants remember specific incidents in an experience, and relate to the group one particular incident that was memorable for them.

Population: Children through adults.

Group Size: Under 20.

Time: 15–30 minutes.

Activity Level: Low.

Goals

- To help participants remember the sequence of events that happened during an experience.
- To help participants solidify one event that had particular significance for them.

Materials: None.

Procedure: Ask the participants to sit in a circle. Explain that you want them to think of the previous experience as if they had viewed it with a video camera. Have them rewind the film to the beginning of the experience, then play the film in their minds, seeing different events that happened during the experience.

Explain to the group that when they have replayed the film in their minds, to go back and choose one frame that was especially memorable. Have the group visualize that this frame will be taken out of the movie, printed, framed, and hung in a place of the individual's choice. Invite each individual to explain to the group what picture was chosen, why it was memorable, and where it will hang.

Thoughts: At times I have asked groups to pick a frame from their movie that has specific meaning in terms of their leadership, their being a successful group member, something they noticed about someone else in the group, etc. Framing the activity in this way can move it in a specific direction.

The Whip

Description: This reflective exercise allows a group to quickly share an insight from a learning experience. It also provides the opportunity for people to "pass" and return to reflective thoughts once given additional time for reflection.

Population: Children through adults.

Group Size: 1-50. It gets a bit long after 50 people.

Time: Three to five minutes, with possible extensions into other associated reflective activities.

Activity Level: Low.

Goals

- To get a quick insight into how group members briefly describe a learning experience.
- To share these brief insights with other group members in a group setting.

Materials: None.

Procedure: Following an activity, ask the group to form a circle where everyone can see one another. Once this is established, ask group members to think of one word that describes the past activity for them (e.g., an adjective) that they are willing to share with the group. People are given about 30 to 60 seconds to think of this word before beginning to share. Tell the group that after the first person volunteers his or her response, the whip will move counterclockwise around the circle allowing each person to share the one word response. Let people know that if it is their turn and they are not ready to answer, they can say "pass" and the group will come back to them later in the activity.

Once everyone has answered, the facilitator has several options: 1) the group can move on to another activity with these thoughts in mind, 2) group members can expand on the word they offered, or 3) group members can ask clarification questions to other individuals based on their responses. The option(s) taken will depend upon the participants' needs and time considerations.

Thoughts: This is a good "warm-up" reflection exercise for clients, particularly with young children. It seems to stimulate thinking for more focused and longer reflective exercises in the future.

The questions the group responds to can also be more focused around a particular learning, group response, or interaction. Examples can include:

- Choose one word or short phrase that describes your contribution to the group in the learning experience.
- Select a person in the group and state a word or short phrase that describes his or her contribution to the group in the learning experience.
- Think of a key time in the learning experience that you think was pivotal for the group in the learning experience and share that with the group.

The more interactive and reciprocal the comments, the more likely the facilitator will need to extend the discussion to cover the meanings of the comments.

Weather Report

Description: A creative technique for participants to explain their experience by relating it to some aspect of the weather.

Population: Children through adults.

Time: Fifteen minutes, depending on the size of the group.

Activity Level: Low.

Goals

- To have participants share their experiences and feelings about an activity.
- To allow participants the opportunity to make metaphorical connections between their experiences and the weather.

Materials: None.

Procedure: As the facilitator, you might say: "I would like you to give us a weather report of your experience. Was it sunny, temperatures in the 70s, and a slight breeze out of the west, or was it partly cloudy with a chance of storms in the late afternoon? What weather best describes what happened to you during this activity? Why did you choose that particular weather?"

Thoughts: The basic structure of the activity can be used with a variety of topics. I have asked: "What vegetable/dessert/car/musical instrument were you in this activity?"

I have also obtained a variety of paint chip samples from a paint store and used them in several ways. "Choose the chip that represents your experience and tell us why you chose that color." Or "choose a chip that shows how you felt at the beginning of the activity and another one that shows how you feel now."

Another possibility is to present the group with a selection of stones from a river, shells from the beach, or twigs from the woods. Ask them to choose one that represents their experience, and describe it to the group. My best experience with this exercise is when I picked up small rocks from a peak that the group had struggled to climb. The students immediately knew where the rocks had come from, and were appreciative of the connection between their accomplishment and the rocks. Years later, students tell me that they still have their rock in a cherished place.

Reflection Activities

**Post-Experience
(Props Involved)**

Carabiner Connections

Description: This closure experience has several valuable features. It takes advantage of the analogous similarities between a carabiner's functions and a participant's functions as a group member. A second feature is that it can serve as a clear "mark of closure" and "moving on" activity when done in the manner presented. In working with groups, it has always been a bit uncomfortable for people to end their experience by saying "See ya later—have a great life." This reflective learning experience addresses this issue and allows group members to approach closure in open and healthy manner. This also may serve to eliminate many of regression issues commonly observed in groups during the termination or separation stage of group development (Priest & Gass, 1997).

Population: Children through adults. Groups comfortable dialoguing in metaphors may benefit more from the debriefing than other groups, but this may not be a limiting factor. It is best used with groups that have been together for a period of time and are in the process of separating.

Group Size: 1-20. Eight to 12 people seem best, although smaller numbers work quite well.

Time: Dependent on the number of people, but plan for about 10 minutes organizational time plus 10 minutes per person in the group.

Activity Level: Low.

Goals

- To acknowledge and celebrate the completion of a group experience.
- To provide a clear and healthy point of closure for individuals in groups, particularly if these group members won't see each other again.
- To identify individual successes and allow others to acknowledge these successes.
- To present clients with a carabiner as a representation of their efforts and accomplishments, particularly how they might use or apply these gains as members of future groups.

Materials

One "toy" carabiner per person (a couple of extras in case you mis-count can avoid problems!!!). Carabiners that take on representa-tion of the participants' learning (e.g., words imprinted on the carabiner representing the group or carabiners in a variety of col-ors) can have enriching applications.

Procedure: Ask the group to sit in a circle and place the carabiners in the center of the circle. Have the carabiners interconnected with one another in a "necklace" style fashion. Unclip a carabiner and begin talking about its qualities and how these may often relate to people. Some common examples include:

- carabiners (like people) are incredibly strong when taking a load in certain positions and directions (e.g., 2200-2800 kg) and in other positions are much weaker and can break;
- carabiners are incredibly strong when they (their gates) are closed, but will only work with others (pieces of equipment like ropes) when they are open, which is when they are most vulnerable;
- while strong as an individual piece of equipment, carabiners are often used in pairs, in complimentary positions, in order for them to be truly capable of accomplishing their tasks;
- different types and shapes of carabiners (e.g., locking, non-locking, dogleg) work well in different situations, and it is not so much which carabiner is "better," but which carabiner works best in a particular situation.

At this time, re-clip the carabiner used for the previous discus-sion back into the carabiner chain in the middle of the circle. Ask participants to consider how the carabiners, like themselves as group members, become connected, disconnected, and recon-nected in their lives. Some of these connections are long term while others are only for a short time. How they handle these connec-tions, separations, and reconnections may have a lot to do with how they successfully progress in life.

Explain that this group, like others they have experienced in the past and will experience in the future, is coming to an end. To acknowledge and celebrate the group's accomplishments, ask each person to consider the triumphs, gains, goals, etc. that individual members have been able to achieve with the group's assistance. With this consideration, invite group members to disconnect a car-abiner from the ones linked together in the middle of the circle and present it to another group member as a symbol of their being, effort, and accomplishment in the group experience. In this presentation, the presenter, as well as other group members, are encouraged to add comments on why this person is receiving this carabiner. If the recipient has any clarification questions on the comments they are hearing, they are encouraged to respond. Other than these comments, participants are asked to listen to what is being given to them in terms of verbal gifts.

After all of the carabiners have been given out, ask individuals to stand up and join hands. Explain how this group is ending and ask people to acknowledge the special experiences of being a member of the group. Then invite group members to turn away from the group (i.e., turn 180 degrees so that their backs are facing away from the group). Encourage them to acknowledge that the group is over and that while reconnections will be made, people are moving on to future experiences. Ask individuals to plant this group experience in an appropriate place in their memory. When this is completed, participants are invited to turn back around and gather their things to leave.

Thoughts: I generally use this with groups who have been together for longer periods of time, however, it can be done with groups that are together only for a day or so if they have previous "connections" or history with one another. Other thoughts I add to the group during this experience depend upon the group's and individual member's needs. A comment that I often include about small groups is one from Margaret Mead, stating basically that it isn't that small groups have not accomplished social change in our time together as human beings; in fact, such groups are the only way such change has occurred in society.

Circle of Rope[1]

Description: This activity helps individuals acknowledge what they have learned from an experience and process their feelings around the breakup of the group.

Population: Older youth through adult.

Group Size: 8-15.

Time: Fifteen minutes to an hour, depending on the size of the group.

Activity Level: Low.

Goals

- To help individuals recognize what they learned from an experience.
- To give individuals an opportunity to verbalize what learning they will take with them from the experience.
- To introduce the idea of the separation of the group members.
- To provide a means for individuals to stay connected to the experience.

Materials

- One length of rope, such as a retired climbing rope (1 foot per person).
- One sharp knife.

Procedure: Tie the rope in a circle with an overhand knot and have the group sit or stand in a circle holding on to the rope.

Talk to the group about how the rope represents the group, using words and phrases such as "connected," "linked," and "joined together." If the rope was used during the experience, talk about how it was part of the experience and how its use helped in the group's success. If the rope was not used during the experience, talk about its history and different uses, and how it is now representing the group. Link the history of the rope to the individual histories of participants and how they are joined together as a group with the rope.

Introduce the idea that the experience is ending and each person will be breaking from the group and going his or her separate

---

[1]This activity originally appeared in *Ziplines*, No. 36, Summer, 1998

end when they separate. Each person learned and shared with others in the group and they will take the learning and memories away from the experience. Those memories will keep individuals connected to the experience and to the other group members.

Ask individuals in the group to think of a specific, important learning that they will take with them when they leave. After giving them a few minutes to think, cut off a piece of the rope with the knife. Explain what you will be taking with you from the course, and then pass the knife to the person next to you. That person cuts off a piece of the rope and talks about the important learning they will take with them and passes the knife on. The knife gets passed around the circle, with each person cutting a piece off and sharing the learning that he or she will take away.

When the knife has returned to you, reinforce the idea that the group will be separating and individuals have a piece of the rope to take with them to help them remember the experience and the learning they have had.

Thoughts: I like this activity because it gives each member of the group a chance to reflect and verbalize what was meaningful and important. The piece of rope has metaphorical meanings for each person. I have several pieces of rope hanging in my office that remind me of specific courses and experiences and what I learned from each.

Continuum Exercises

Description: These activities allow the group to experientially rank an experience based on a question posed by the facilitator. The process makes it possible for individuals to see where others in the group placed themselves on the continuum and for each person to express why he or she chose a particular spot.

Population: Children through adults. The technique can be adapted for various age levels.

Group Size: 1-20.

Time: Fifteen to thirty minutes, depending on the level of follow-up questions.

Activity Level: Low.

Goals

- To assess the attitudes/opinions/feelings of each group member following a learning experience.
- To assess the effectiveness of a learning experience.
- To heighten the group awareness around each individual's evaluation of the learning experience.

Materials

- One piece of 8X10 paper for each member of the group.
- Markers.

Procedure: Presented below is two ways of facilitating this activity.

At the beginning of an experience, have the group members identify group goals for the experience. Ask members of the group to write the goals on the sheets of paper, one goal per sheet. After the experience is completed, choose two stationary endpoints, such as two trees that are in line with each other. Identify one tree as "absolute success," and the other tree as "dismal failure." Have the group place the sheets of paper in between the two points, based on their assessment of how well the group accomplished the goals written on the paper. Individuals are able to move sheets to different locations, depending on their assessment of that goal.

An example of a follow up question includes "What can we do to move the goals near the "dismal failure" end of the continuum closer to the "absolute success" end?"

Prior to the experience, the facilitator can write the numbers 1–10 on sheets of paper, one number per sheet. After the experience, lay down the numbers in number order between two endpoints, as in the exercise above. Ask a specific question pertaining to the experience, and ask individuals to place themselves on a number that represents their answer to the question. Be sure to identify which number represents "the best" and which number represents "not so good." Follow up questions may revolve around why individuals chose to put themselves on a particular number, and what needs to be done in order for them to change to a better number.

Deck of Cards

Description: The use of a simple deck of playing cards gives individuals the opportunity to express successes and difficulties from an experience, and what they noticed about themselves and others in the group.

Population: Children through adults.

Group Size: Up to 20 works best.

Time: Twenty to thirty minutes.

Goals

- To give students an opportunity to express their feelings about success and difficulties in an experience.
- To give students an opportunity to express their feelings about a group member.
- To allow students to reflect on their learning from an experience.

Materials: A deck of playing cards.

Activity Level: Low.

Procedure: Designate a meaning to each suit within the deck of cards. For example hearts could represent successes, spades could represent situations individuals had a difficult time with, diamonds could represent something they noticed about themselves and clubs could represent something they noticed about one of the other group members.

Shuffle the deck and deal each individual a hand (up to 8 cards). For each card, the individual shares with the group an example of what the suit represents. The numbers on the cards and face cards can be involved also. For example, Jacks are wild cards that can be traded for another card in the deck and the numbers on the cards represent how many thoughts that individual may share with the group, etc. You may want to "stack the deck" with specific cards or adapt the rules so that the person who draws a "10" does not have to share 10 items—this could get a bit lengthy!

Thoughts: I have seen this activity done with M&M's also. The facilitator passed around a bag of candy and invited participants to take as many as they wanted. She then explained that each color had a particular meaning, and that individuals could share their thoughts and feelings based on the number of M&M's they had of a specific color. For example, if an individual had 4 green M&M's, he or she would share 4 things they learned during the experience. After they had shared, they could eat the M&M's!

Fan Mail

Description: This is a powerful activity in which people participate in thoughtful and personal reflection by writing a letter to themselves. This activity can be done toward the end of an experience or whenever participants have quiet time to think and reflect. After the experience, they receive the letter in the mail as a reminder of their thoughts during the experience.

Population: Anyone can participate in this activity.

Group Size: Any size group.

Time: This may depend on the attention span of the participants. It may also depend on the length of experience and the timing of the activity within the experience. For example, if participants are involved in a month-long experience and writing a letter during a solo, then sometime during that two-day solo period the letter will be written. If participants are involved in a one-day program, then 20 minutes at the end of the day could also work.

Activity Level: Low.

Goals

- To assist participants in reflecting on their experiences.
- To provide participants with a reminder of their learning and personal thoughts during an experience.

Materials: Participants will need a notebook or some paper, a pen or pencil, and a stamped envelope that they will address to themselves.

Procedure: Explain to students that they will be writing a letter to themselves that will be mailed to them at a future date. Give them guidelines about what you want them to write about: their experiences; their future goals; changes they have seen in themselves; specifics that they have learned through the experience, etc. Depending on the group, the instructor may want to provide participants with some focused open-ended questions to aid in the reflection process.

   After participants have written the letter, give them envelopes to address, put their letters in, and seal before giving them to you. This is an assurance that their "fan mail" will only be read by them. Collect their letters when they are done writing, and put the letters in a place where they will not be lost! Mail the letters at a later date (two weeks, one month, six months, etc.).

Thoughts: During longer experiences, I have had participants write a letter to themselves during the first day of our time together and then I have given the letters to them at the end of the experience. As a group, we then talk about participants' expectations, fears, goals, courage, growth, etc. as a way of reflecting on each individual's experience within the group.

Friendship Pin

Description: Participants choose beads that represent their experience and put them on a large pin that they can attach to their clothes.

Population: Children through adult.

Group Size: Any size group.

Time: Up to an hour, depending on the group size.

Activity Level: Low.

Goals

- To give students an opportunity to reflect on and express what they learned during an experience.
- To give students an opportunity to give feedback to another person in the group.

Materials

- Small beads of various colors, shapes, and/or textures.
- One large pin for each person (a baby diaper pin or kilt pin work well).

Procedure: Ask the group to choose a bead that represents their experience for them, or represents how they achieved their goals for the experience. Depending on how big the pins are and how small the beads are, you may want to ask two or three questions. Pass out a small piece of paper with a name of a person from the group on it to each individual. Have participants choose a bead that represents that person for them.

When everyone is ready, one person starts by showing their beads and explaining their meaning pertaining to the questions asked. The person in the group who received that person's name follows by giving them the bead and explaining why they chose it. The first person puts the beads on the pin and attaches it to his or her clothing somewhere.

Thoughts: The more creative the beads are, the more creativity participants can put into their meaning.

Gifts

Description: Gifts are a wonderful way for the giver to express feelings about a person and for the receiver to obtain feedback about himself or herself. The activity works best when students have time to get to know their receiver well.

Population: Children through adults.

Group Size: Up to 20 works best.

Time: Dependent on number of people, plan on 5 minutes per person.

Goals

- To give students an opportunity to express their feelings about a group member.
- To give students an opportunity to receive feedback about themselves.
- To allow students a creative outlet for expression.

Materials: None. Students will find materials on their own.

Activity Level: Low.

Procedure: Have participants choose someone in the group to receive their present. You might put everyone's name in a hat and have each person pick a name out of the hat. Do this during the beginning of an experience so students have ample time to make their presents.

Explain that at the end of the trip or course they will be giving a present to the person whose name they drew. The present should be a gift that says something about that person. It is important to not let that person know who the gift giver is, and important to get to know that person well so that the gift is meaningful. The gift must be made from natural materials, and not include anything that they brought with them. Individuals may ask for help from anyone in the group, and must make the present themselves.

The last night of the course, gather the group in a circle. Take turns giving out presents, explaining the meaning behind each gift.

Thoughts: I am always touched at the thought and creativity that goes into each gift. I have also done this activity with imaginary gifts. I will say to a group, after they have chosen names, "Imagine that you are giving this person a box. Inside the box is something that they may need or desire that only you can give to them. What does the box look like? What is in the box? Why are you giving it?"

This puts a different twist on the activity, and is more of an abstract exercise than the concrete presents. It allows students to use their imaginations and come up with creative ideas. This can be done on the spur of the moment and does not need the advance preparation of the presents from natural materials.

Headlines

Description: In this activity, participants act as reporters and create a headline and picture for the front page of the local newspaper based on the activity the group just completed.

Population: Children through adults

Group Size: Any size will work, and realize that a large group will take longer to finish the activity.

Time: Fifteen minutes for drawing, five minutes per small group for discussion.

Goals

- To give students an opportunity to verbalize an important aspect of their experience.
- To use visual means as a processing technique.

Materials

- Paper about the size of the front page of a newspaper.
- Markers.

Activity Level: Low.

Procedure: Give each participant (or pair of individuals) a piece of paper. Make the colored markers available to everyone.

Explain to the group that they are reporters from the local newspaper and have been observing the group completing the latest activity. They are to imagine that they took a picture of the activity that will go on the front page of today's edition. What would the picture be? Instruct them to draw the picture on the paper. They also need to write a headline that will explain the picture and give the essence of the activity for the newspaper's readers.

Give students 15 minutes to complete their headlines, then have them share what they created.

Thoughts: If possible, hang up the papers in a public space. The pictures and headlines are a wonderful reminder for participants of their experience.

Keepsake

Description: This activity allows individuals to reflect and think metaphorically about their experiences. It also provides participants with a tangible reminder of their experience and their learning.

Population: Children through adults.

Group Size: Any size is fine. Of course, the larger the group, the longer this activity takes unless the larger groups are broken up into smaller groups of 10-12. Larger groups tend to be less intimate than smaller groups.

Time: Variable depending on number of participants and how long each one of them speaks.

Activity Level: Low.

Goals

- To assist participants in reflecting on their experiences by looking at the "big picture."
- To allow the participants to make metaphorical connections between their experiences and a special object gathered during their experience.
- To have the participants share thoughts regarding their experience.
- To provide participants with a tangible reminder of their experience and their learning.

Materials: Participants bring their own materials to the circle.

Procedure: During an experience, ask each participant to look for an object that represents her/his experience. Let the participants know they need to keep this object with them and, therefore, it should be small. When it is time to do the activity, have participants sit in a circle and explain how the objects they chose represent their experience. Everyone speaks one at a time with no interruptions.

Thoughts: This activity can be valuable at different times during an experience:

- This is a good activity to do at the end of an experience since it can offer some closure.
- It can also be done half way through an experience as a "check in."
- If there is one day that will be especially enlightening, demanding, or unique for the group, you could ask participants to find an object that represents their experience that day.

Variations and important considerations:

- A variation is that the leader can collect objects from a special place that the group has been (e.g., a mountain peak, a tough river crossing, a field trip) and have participants choose one of those objects that represents their experience and describe it to the group. My best experience with this variation is when I picked up small rocks during a four-mile canoe portage that the group had struggled through. The students immediately knew where the rocks came from, and were appreciative of the connection between their accomplishment and the rocks. Years later, students tell me that they still have their rock in a cherished place.
- In many natural areas, we live by the motto, "Take only pictures, leave only footprints" (and hopefully not too many footprints!). In an effort to "leave no trace," leaders may have to set some guidelines around acceptable objects depending on the group of participants. Also, this activity may only work in certain areas.
- One participant chose a sprinkler system at a nearby challenge course. He explained that this sprinkler system represented his experience in that lots of knowledge (water) was disseminated and shared, and that the experience had helped him and the group (and the grass) grow! While the rest of the participants put their rocks or acorns in their pockets, this participant decided to draw the sprinkler system so that he would have a concrete reminder of his experience since he couldn't take the object with him. Drawing is always an option!

Lessons from Light

Description: Candles are used in this activity as a means for students to express lessons they learned from an experience.

Population: Older youths to adults.

Group Size: A smaller group (10-12) will work best.

Time: Depending on the size of group, give yourself a good hour.

Goals

- To give students an opportunity to reflect on what they learned during an experience.
- To give students a means to express themselves concerning what they learned.

Materials

- One large candle for the center of the circle.
- Enough smaller candles of different colors for each person in the group.

Activity Level: Low.

Procedure: Instruct the group to sit in a circle. Give each individual a small candle. Place the large candle in the middle of the circle.

As you light the large candle, you can begin to talk about the experience the group completed. Have the group members talk about the events of the experience. Questions to ask might include "What happened when we first arrived? What happened the next day? What happened after that?" The purpose of these questions is to help individuals remember the experience. Sometimes so much happens on an experience, that individuals forget details. The questions will help them remember the sequence as well as the details of the experience.

The next step is for you to choose one of the members of the group, give them your small candle, and explain why the color of that candle suits that person. They in turn will select someone to pass their candle on to, giving positive reasons why the color matches the person. No one should be selected twice, and by the end, all the candles will be distributed to the group members with meaning behind each one. Explain that the large candle represents the group and the experience, and the small candles represent the participants as individuals.

Then, ask group members to think of something important they learned during the experience, a lesson that they will take with them. Ask for a volunteer to begin, and have him or her light their candle from the large candle in the center of the circle. After they sit down, have them explain to the group the lesson they are taking with them. Either proceed around the circle from that person, or popcorn around the group.

Thoughts: Participants can take the candle with them as a reminder of the lessons from the experience. When they light the candle at home they will remember the experience and what they learned.

This activity is adapted from David Weissman and Sara Teel.

Obstacles to Change

Description: The goal of many programs is to help participants make changes in their lives. It is sometimes difficult for participants to leave a program with a clear idea of how they will maintain the changes they may have accomplished as a result of the program. This activity helps participants identify the obstacles in their lives that may stand in the way of their successful change.

Population: Children through adults.

Group Size: Any size group, depending on the discussion desired.

Time: Variable depending on program goals.

Activity Level: Low.

Goals

- To help participants identify obstacles that may interfere with their intended change.

Materials: None.

Procedure: Participants are reminded that one of the goals of the program is to be able to transfer changes in behavior or thoughts that resulted from the program, back to the "real" life circumstances the participant comes from. In order for participants to be successful in transferring their change they need to begin to anticipate some of the barriers that may interfere with their change.

Ask participants to sit in a comfortable position and close their eyes. Have them think of one change that will make their life better. The facilitator can use his or her understanding of the group to suggest a few possible changes. Ask the participants to imagine they are on a road in a beautiful wooded peaceful setting. They are walking down this road on their way to receive praise from a large group of people who have been assembled to celebrate their success in making the change. As they are almost to the awaiting crowd, something or someone jumps in front of them and will not let them pass to receive the praise they deserve. Ask the participants to identify who or what this block might be.

After participants have identified their block, ask them to break into small groups and discuss what might stand in their way. After they have discussed the obstacles, ask the participants to help each other design strategies to move beyond these obstacles.

Thoughts: Depending on the group of participants, this can be an emotional and high-powered activity. Often a father or mother is the identified obstacle, or excessive drinking might be mentioned. The facilitator should be reminded that the solutions to remove the obstacle are very important and should be shared out loud. By allowing all members of the group to listen to how each individual intends to solve a problem, the entire group gains new insight and direction regarding how to successfully make changes.

Pat on the Back

Description: This reflective technique is typically used as a closure activity, having group members focus on what they have done well and reasons for success. It is an interactive experience where positive synergy can create wonderful insights for people.

Population: I have used it most often with children and family groups, but it also has some applications to less formal adult groups.

Group Size: 10-no limit. With this experience, more people isn't a problem as long as people know each other well enough to provide feedback or even congratulations, and as long as there are enough facilitators present to support positive processes. It probably works best with groups of 15-45.

Time: The way the activity is described here, it would take approximately 20 to 40 minutes. It can be shorter if only certain portions of the reflective learning experience are used.

Activity Level: Low.

Goals

- To highlight positive gains experienced by an individual from group members.
- To self-identify, with group support, elements that contribute to a person's successes.
- To heighten the group awareness around individual learning.
- To provide group members with the opportunity to congratulate one another on their accomplishments.

Materials: Paper plates, small point markers (at least one per person plus five or so extra), and masking tape. Be sure that the markers are NOT the kind that will soak through the paper plates and leave permanent marks on the surface underneath! A marker board or flip chart outlining instructions is often helpful for people.

Procedure: Assemble the group and ask each person to take a paper plate and a marker. After this has been done, ask them to carefully trace their hand on the plate with their fingers separated comfortably.

For fun, ask how many people have refrigerators at home (most folks do; if you are working with a client group that does not, choose a more appropriate reference). As people raise their hands in agreement, ask them what the door(s) of their refrigerator look like. A typical response is that the doors are covered with important notes that serve as a kind of "bulletin board." Tell the group that they will be creating an important piece of work to add to their refrigerator collection.

Next, instruct the group to take their plates and write a word or short phrase on each finger of the drawn hand. The words are to pertain to the group's time together, with the following meanings:

- Index finger ("pointer")—A direction or goal that you want to point yourself toward in your future.
- Middle finger ("tall")—Your biggest accomplishment during the learning experience.
- Ring finger ("commitment")—What you do as an individual to help you stay committed to reaching your future goal.
- Little finger ("pinkie")—The time you had the most fun during the learning experience.
- Thumb—A time when you received a "thumbs up" from the group that you were proud of.

Have people take time to write the words or phrases on each of the corresponding fingers of their traced handprint. Encourage people to do this in the groups that they worked with during the day or are a part of in their lives (e.g., families).

Once this is completed, ask everyone to take the plate and tape it on his or her back. Give people an appropriate length of time (10 minutes or so) to go around to others in the group and write notes of thanks and congratulations on the part of the plate outside of the hand. The notes should pertain to something the person was able to accomplish during the learning experience or thoughts of encouragement as this person continues on from the learning experience.

Once the positive "synergy" of the exercise is going, people usually have little difficulty sharing with others by writing on the backs of their group mates. It's fun to watch "long lines" of folks all writing on each other's backs at the same time and interesting how the comments of one person feed on the thoughts of another. There also is an interesting interaction between the five points the individual wrote inside the hand, and what others write in support.

After the writing time is up, ask people to take the plates off their backs, and read and share the comments they received. Sometimes I do a quick "whip around" the group and let each person share one or two things that he or she is particularly proud of. And of course, people are encouraged to take the plate home and put it on their refrigerator.

Thoughts: With families or other "system" type of groups, another step I add to the sequence is to have them create a mobile out of the plates and decide on an appropriate spot to hang the plates in their home or office. This can punctuate the connection that exists between each person's accomplishments, goals, and the rest of the system.

For clients with indicating psychological issues (e.g., where being touched by random people on your back is not OK), instead of having people tape the plate to their backs, I have them pass their plate around and "fill their plate" with compliments and reinforcing statements from group members.

Photo Album

Description: One of the end results of this activity is that an intact group of participants has a photo album to take back to the office, classroom etc. The reflective process of having a group create a photo album may be enhanced by talking about their experiences during/after they have created the album. This way, the photo album serves as the tangible reflection tool, (the "what" as in "what happened"), and the conversation could focus on transferring knowledge and planning for the future (the "so what" and the "now what" phases).

Population: Children through adult. Intact groups are nice since they can have one photo album for all of them to see and share. If groups are not intact, color copied photo albums is always an option.

Group Size: Best for small to medium sized groups (maximum 20)

Time: This depends on number of photographs and how creative and detailed participants want to make their photo album.

Activity Level: Low.

Goals

- To assist participants in reflecting on their experiences.
- To have the participants share thoughts regarding their experience with other group members.
- To provide participants with a tangible representation of their experience and their learning.

Materials: Cameras and film (disposable cameras are an option if participants do not have their own cameras), a one hour photo developing store nearby, a photo album (or a hard backed blank book), pens, cartoon conversation balloon stickers and hopefully some grant money for all the materials and film developing!

Procedure: At the beginning of an experience, make sure everyone has a camera. Pass out disposable cameras to those participants who don't have their own. Tell the group they are to document their experience together; to capture all the unforgettable moments ... It can be framed in many ways depending on what your group goals are.

At the end of the experience (or close to it) you will need to gather all the film together and run to a one-hour photo-developing store! In the mean time, if the group members have been keeping journals, they could reflect on the experience while writing in their journals. Depending on the population, you might want to ask them to write about a few directed questions to aid in their reflection.

When the photos come back, it's time for the group to create their photo album. During this time, you could take advantage of some teachable moments related to a few specific photographs. You could also wait until the photo album is complete to talk about the experience as a whole, what it meant for the participants, what they are going to do with what they learned, and how it transfers into their lives.

Thoughts: There are many ways to frame the idea of the photo album, and lots of ways to process the group's experience through the use of the photo album. Each will depend on the populations with which you are working. You may choose to carefully frame and debrief this activity and experience, or you may choose to let the process of creating the photo album serve as a tool for reflection with the direction for discussion decided by the group.

Pinning Ceremony

Description: The most common reflective exercises are closure experiences, and the most typical closure experiences from learning situations are graduation ceremony experiences. The reflective exercise outlined here mirrors this ritual. This particular experience has many connections from Outward Bound programs, but it has multiple applications and uses for a variety of groups.

Population: Children through adults. Tailoring it to have particular meaning for specific participant characteristics generally adds meaning to the experience.

Group Size: 1-20. It should probably be done in separate smaller groups if the numbers are larger than 20.

Time: Dependent on the number of people, but plan for about 5 minutes organizational time plus 5 minutes per person in the group.

Activity Level: Low.

Goals

- To acknowledge and celebrate the completion of an experience.
- To identify individual successes.
- To present participants with a pin as a token representation of their efforts and accomplishments.

Materials: One pin per person (having a couple of extra can avoid problems). Having pins that take on symbolic representation of the clients' learning is suggested.

Procedure: Prior to the experience, purchase/gather symbolic pins for participants. Examples of symbolism that I have used have included "apple" pins for teachers and animal pins for wilderness experiences. These pins can be purchased at a variety of stores and can be quite beautiful and intricate (when I have found a particularly good store, I tend to "stock up" my supply). Some organizations actually have pins that are custom-made of their organizational emblem and motto.

With participants sitting in a circle, facilitate a general overview and summary of your experience. You might include inspirational readings. The concepts and ideas shared at this time generally focus on the learning and experiences shared together and possible thoughts on how this will continue to stay with everyone once they go their separate ways. Toward the end of this dialogue, take the time to spread out the pins in front of everyone and allow them to examine them (for the purposes of this discussion, I will use animal pins). People see an eagle, fox, bear, chickadee, salmon, badger, etc. as some of the pins in the collection. While they are examining the pins, inform participants that they will give and receive one of these from the group as part of their graduation from the learning experience.

After people view the pins, ask them to consider who should receive which pin. Participants are invited to present a pin to a person as a symbol of their being, effort, and accomplishment in the learning experience. After stating the presentation, other group members may add additional comments as "gifts" to the person receiving the pin. If the recipient has any clarification questions on the comments they are hearing, they are encouraged to respond. Other than these comments, participants usually focus on listening to what is being given to them in terms of verbal gifts.

Thoughts: I generally use this with groups who have been together for a long period of time (at least 10 days if not more). If the pins are all the same, comments seem more unified and similar. If they are different, comments are more symbolic around the characteristics shared with the pin. Given this, identical pins seem to make more sense for groups who don't know each other well, different pins for groups who do.

These pins often take on great significance for the participant and are often worn or harbored in places of value. Often times participants include me in their pinning ceremonies and when appropriate, has been a great way for participants to provide me with feedback and has given me good feelings about what we've been able to accomplish as a group together.

Postcards

Description: The use of picture postcards helps group members identify feelings around an experience.

Population: Children through adults—works well with younger groups, because it is a structured, visual way of expressing feelings.

Time: Thirty minutes, depending on the size of the group.

Activity Level: Low.

Goals

- To give participants the opportunity to identify their feelings about an experience.
- To have participants share their feelings about an experience with the group.

Materials: A variety of picture postcards, either colored or black and white.

Procedure: After an experience, lay the picture postcards out in front of the group and have individuals look them over quickly. Pose a question related to the experience such as "What was it like for you having to trust the other group members in this experience?" Give the individuals time to look more closely at the postcards and to choose one that represents their answer to the question.

When everyone has chosen a postcard, go around and have each group member explain why he or she chose that particular postcard and what the picture means in relation to the experience and the question posed.

Thoughts: Other methods of accomplishing the same goals as this exercise exist. You might find pictures and/or words in magazines that depict a variety of emotions and paste them on 3X5 note cards. Check out equipment catalogs and bookstores for other sources of cards.

Puzzle Feedback

Description: This activity is a structured opportunity for participants to give each other feedback. The feedback is written on small puzzle pieces which fit together to form a puzzle.

Population: Older populations, from young adult on.

Time: Several hours to a full day, depending on group size and commitment level.

Activity Level: Low.

Goals

- To have participants give each other feedback.
- To give participants an opportunity to practice giving and receiving feedback.

Materials: One small puzzle for each participant. Make sure that there are enough puzzle pieces in each puzzle for every participant to write feedback on one piece. For example, if the group size is 10, you will need 10 puzzles that each have at least 10 pieces. I have purchased puzzles at craft stores and art supply stores.

Procedure: Prior to this activity, have participants write down feedback for each person in the group; one thing that they have noticed about the person that has been positive, and one thing that they see as a challenge to that person. An example might be: "You have good ideas which help the group accomplish our tasks, and I challenge you to speak up more." Also prior to this activity, teach the skills of giving and receiving feedback.

On the day of the activity, pass out a puzzle to each person. One person volunteers to go first, and passes out their puzzle pieces to the group, one piece for each person. Each group member writes their feedback for that person on the puzzle piece; positive on one side, challenge on the other side. When everyone is finished, one group member begins by telling the person the feedback on the puzzle piece, then gives the piece to him or her. This continues until everyone has given the person their feedback. The process continues with each person in the group.

Thoughts: One plus to this activity is that each group member has a written record of the feedback received that they can revisit at any future time. I give each person a small plastic bag to put the puzzle in so that they can keep track of the small pieces.

The idea of the puzzle pieces fitting together to form a whole can be used metaphorically by the instructor. The activity can also be a good jumping place to discuss topics such as: how we view ourselves and how others view us, how it feels to give and receive feedback, etc.

I have found this activity to be emotionally draining for group members. Be aware that issues may come up and that this activity may be difficult for some individuals.

Quilt

Description: Designing, creating individual pieces, and putting together a group quilt has many metaphorical meanings pertaining to a group and individuals within that group. It is also a wonderful visual representation of the group.

Population: Children through adults.

Group Size: 10-15.

Time: Several hours, depending on the complexity of the project.

Activity Level: Low.

Goals

- To help participants express in an artistic manner the part of the experience that was meaningful for them.
- To portray in a visual means the joining together of individuals to form a group.

Materials: The materials needed for this exercise can range from very simple to very complex, depending on how the exercise is organized. For simple quilts use construction paper, marking pens, and tape. For more complex quilts use fabric, fabric markers, sewing notions (a sewing machine helps too!). There are also markers available that participants use to draw on paper, then the image is ironed onto a piece of fabric. Check with a local craft store for more information about making quilts.

Procedure: After an experience, have individuals in the group draw a picture of a particularly memorable event for them. You might want to direct them in a certain way with statements such as "Draw a picture of yourself when you felt the happiest; when you felt a part of the group; when you felt like you were a leader; etc."
When group members are done drawing, have them present their picture to the rest of the group. Have them explain the picture and why that particular event was important to them. Connect the pictures into a quilt, outlining each picture with construction paper or fabric. Hang the quilt in a place where group members can see it and relive the experience.

Thoughts: I used this exercise with a group of Brownies who were in kindergarten and just starting out in Girl Scouts. It was one of the most memorable activities we did. Every year thereafter, until the girls were in 6th grade, we would pull out the quilt. We would look at the pictures the girls had drawn and have a discussion about how they had grown and changed, how our group had changed, and what goals we had for the coming year. It was a wonderful metaphor for the girls as individuals and as group members.

Spider Web

Description: In this activity, participants thank other group members while passing a ball of yarn around the group.

Population: Children to adults.

Time: Thirty to forty-five minutes based on a group of 10-12 people.

Activity Level: Low.

Goals

* To give students an opportunity to give and receive feedback.

Materials

* One ball of yarn or light string.

Procedure: Explain to the participants that they are going to thank other group members for something they did during the experience. One person will start the activity by holding on to the end of a ball of yarn and passing the ball to the person they want to thank. As they pass the ball, they say what it is that they are thanking the person for. That person holds on to the yarn and passes the ball to another person, verbalizing their thanks. It is important to make sure that everyone in the group is included, so you may want to make a rule that each person receives the ball only once.

Thoughts: When the activity is finished, the resulting web is a wonderful metaphor of how each group member is connected to the others in the group by the actions and behaviors of individuals.

The Evolving Evaluation

Description: At the conclusion of a multi-day program this activity has proven to be an effective way for participants to: reflect on their experiences; evaluate the potential transfer of learning; and discuss any unfinished items.

Population: Maturity is the only consideration. This activity works best if the participants are high school age or older.

Group Size: Best for larger groups (+15).

Time: Variable depending on program goals.

Activity Level: Low.

Goals: To help provide an evaluation and summarization process that is conducted by group members and addresses the needs of the group.

Materials: Flip chart paper, masking tape, and markers.

Procedure: Assemble the program group in a comfortable place and explain that they are going to create and run their program evaluation. Remind the group that it is only through careful recollection and reflection that the lessons learned during the program will be transferred and used in the "real world."

Participants are asked to think of particular learning topics that they would be interested in discussing with other group members. In some cases these topics will be related to items that have become clear as a result of the program. In other instances, the topics may relate to items that have been left unattended during the program.

After participants have had a few minutes to collect their thoughts, the leader encourages anyone who would be interested in leading a discussion about one of their topics to take a piece of flip chart paper and write the topic clearly on the paper. After several people have taken a piece of paper, the leader can ask that this round of topics be stopped. Once those interested in leading a discussion have written their topic on their paper, the leader asks each person to hold their paper in front of them and explain to the group the topic and the reason they are interested in discussing this subject.

The leader sets a reasonable amount of time (perhaps 5 minutes) for all participants to collect around the topics they are most interested in discussing. If there is a topic that has little or no inter-est from others, the topic leader is encouraged to join another group. When groups are organized, the leader sets a 20-minute time limit for discussion. Each group should be encouraged to appoint a spokesperson who will report-out the group's discussion at the end of the 20-minute discussion. If there is time and interest the leader can offer another round of topics for discussion. The process for generating these second or third round topics is the same as described earlier.

The primary value of this evaluation exercise is it allows the participants to create the topics and discuss what they feel is important. The topics chosen and the depth of discussion will often surprise the facilitator.

Using Art Materials

Description: Art materials such as markers, colored pencils, clay, colored paper, and natural materials can provide individuals with a creative way to express themselves.

Population: Children through adults.

Group Size: Unlimited.

Time: Varies with materials chosen.

Activity Level: Low.

Goals

- To give students an opportunity to express themselves using the materials available.

Materials

- A variety of art materials, depending on the exercise.

Procedure: The idea behind this exercise is to give participants a question to help them reflect on their learning from an experience, and to allow them to use art materials to express themselves. You might give out paper and markers or colored pencils and have students draw their answer to the question. Or you might give out a large piece of clay and have students sculpt something individually or make a group sculpture. Or you might have a variety of materials such as feathers, colored paper, glue, straws, toothpicks, toilet paper tubes, etc. available and have students make a picture or sculpture. Natural materials such as leaves, sticks, stones, etc. can also be used in pictures and sculptures. The possibilities for creativity are endless!

Thoughts: This is a wonderful way for participants who may not be very verbal or who do not have good writing skills to express themselves about a topic. Questions to ask might include: "What was your favorite part of the activity?"; "What did you learn about yourself?"; or "What did you notice about someone else in the group?" Questions should be based on the age and developmental level of participants.

What's My Learning Style?

Description: At the end of a program it is important for participants to reflect upon what they have learned. It is also very useful for participants to think about how they might have learned during the program. This activity is designed to encourage participants to think about their learning styles: when were they most comfortable and successful as a learner during the program; when were they most impatient or frustrated as a learner during the program?

Population: Best with adults.

Group Size: Any size group, depending on whether participants are asked to share their learning successes/frustrations with other group members.

Time: Twenty minutes for the personal reflection and appropriate time for individuals to share.

Activity Level: Low.

Goals

- To help participants gain a deeper understanding of their preferred and most effective learning styles.
- To encourage participants to take responsibility for creating learning environments that support their styles.

Materials: None.

Procedure: Explain to the group that there are several different ways that people learn "best." Although there is no right or wrong way to learn, some methods are more effective than others for each individual. For example, some people like to read information, some like to talk things over. Whatever process each person uses is fine, provided they have some understanding about how best they learn.

Ask participants to think about the lessons they may have learned during the program. As they reflect upon their learning ask them to write down how they learned these lessons. What techniques were used that helped them learn? What were the characteristics of their learning? After they have had a chance to write down their thoughts about how they learned during the program, ask them to compare this learning with other learning situations in their lives. In what ways was their process/style of learning similar to or different from other situations in which they have learned or are attempting to learn?

After participants have had a chance to see the similarities and differences between learning while on the program and learning away from the program, ask them to construct a plan of action to organize other learning situations so these situations will line-up favorably with their most effective learning style. Ask participants to identify the potential aides and obstacles that might be present when they attempt to change a learning situation.

Thoughts: If time permits, encourage participants to share their reflections, either with the whole group, or in smaller sub-groups. A final reminder to participants that the value of experiential activities is twofold: (1) the new knowledge they may have gained from participating and (2) the ability to examine how they learn. This second benefit, learning how we learn, can be transferred to other learning situations after the program is over.

Wheel of Feelings

Description: This activity is a way for individuals to reflect on and identify feelings regarding an experience.

Population: Children through adults—works well with younger groups, because it is a structured way of expressing feelings.

Time: Thirty minutes, depending on the size of the group.

Activity Level: Low.

Goals

- To give participants the opportunity to identify their feelings about an experience.
- To have participants share their feelings about an experience with the group.

Materials: Wheel of Feelings drawn on a large piece of paper before the group arrives, one place marker for each student (they may pick out their own place marker, say from the environment around them).

The Wheel includes spaces labeled with different feelings ranging from "excited and happy" to "scared and uncomfortable." The labels might vary with the activity. Leave at least one open space where no label is attached so participants may verbalize a feeling they had that is not included in the wheel. The wheel should also include a "safe zone" in the center of the circle to be used if a participant chooses not to share his/her feelings. The rule is that if someone is in the safe zone, no questions or probing is allowed.

Procedure: Create situational questions beforehand that relate to the group's experience together. Questions should be formed so participants get a visual picture of the experience and can identify their feelings during the experience. An example might be: "Remember when you first walked in the room where we were meeting. Who was in the room? Did you know anyone in the room? You brought your pack that was filled with all your gear for the upcoming week. What were you feeling when you set your pack down and sat in your chair?" Move through the experience highlighting key areas of growth for the group: conflicts, challenges, successes, etc.

When the group is ready, describe how the wheel works. You ask a question, group members reflect on the experience relating to the question, recognize how they were feeling during the experience, and put their place marker on the spot on the wheel that matches their feeling. They may use a blank space if their feeling is not listed, and may use the safe zone if they do not feel comfortable sharing their feelings. Each person will have the opportunity to explain to the group why he or she put the place marker in a particular place and what feelings were being experienced. Make sure that everyone understands that the Full Value Contract is in effect during the exercise.

The exercise begins with one of the situational questions previously developed. Group members reflect and then put their place markers on a spot on the wheel. Starting with one person, group members explain why they put their marker on a particular spot and describe how they were feeling at that particular point in time. If appropriate, group members may ask questions to clarify the explanation.

Thoughts: This is a good closure activity to be used at the end of a group experience, as it has the ability to pull together all the various parts of the experience. It can be emotionally charged, with participants expressing feelings that they may have bottled up for the entire experience. The group leader needs to be prepared to facilitate the activity.

In my experience with this activity, people begin by using the labels placed on the wheel. As they become more comfortable with the activity, they begin to develop their own descriptive feeling words for their experience. This is when the real creativity begins!

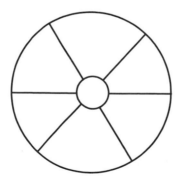

Whose Bandanna Is This?

Description: This debriefing exercise is designed for the middle or end of a group experience where people have enough knowledge about one another to provide some perspective, thoughts, and insight into each other's behaviors. One of its great benefits is that it leaves a "physical reminder" of the experience and associative memories of what has been shared. This debriefing experience works extremely well in groups where individuals can "directly" share information, but it also works in groups where some people may have difficulty sharing or saying what they see in others face-to-face (e.g., some adolescent groups). The wonderful advantage this reflection experience provides is that the reflection and feedback can be owned and stated responsibly "indirectly" through an object.

A quiet, reflective place where all group members can see and hear one another (e.g., circle up in a closed area) and where distractions are kept to a minimum seems to work best.

Population: Children through adults.

Group Size: Anywhere from 8-15 people. Dynamics of the experience will vary with changing group sizes.

Time: This is a long experience! It is dependent upon the number of people, but plan for about 1-2 hours given the focus and discussion that occurs. Don't sell yourself and the group short by not having enough time. Be sure people are ready to sit for a while, and if needed, provide breaks during discussion time.

Activity Level: Low.

Goals

- To have group members discuss and come to a consensus about how each person is seen by the group.
- To provide the group the opportunity to share with each individual person how they are seen by group members and what their contributions have meant to each person.
- To have each individual receive a representative gift from the group with associated meanings.

Materials: At least one bandanna for each group member. Bandannas should include a wide range of colors and designs (note some programs have custom designed bandannas that may not

lend themselves to multiple interpretations). Having 2-3 extra bandannas will make the group experience easier, which may be beneficial or not. As a facilitator, I am always alert for bandanna sales
and sources of colorful and dynamic bandannas. Having a "stash"
of bandannas in your equipment closet is a great idea.

Procedure: Ask everyone to gather in the circle where they can be
comfortable, see each other, and listen to what each person has to
say. Once this circle has been established, place the bandannas in
the middle of the circle and have the group spread them out flat so
that group members may see all of the bandannas.

After this is done, explain to the group that like the differing
bandannas, each person in the group is composed of different elements, designs, and make-ups (choose age appropriate symbolic
words here). The goal of the group is to find the bandanna that best
represents each particular group member, and present this bandanna to this person as a gift from the group. In this process, group
members may see a bandanna they want for themselves, but they
may only *receive* a bandanna that is given to them by the group.

Point out to the group that the giving of a bandanna is done by
consensus. People may propose that a certain bandanna may go to
a person, and the group must dialogue as to why this particular
bandanna goes to a specific person.

Set the ground rules for giving and receiving. The givers
explain to the receiver why the bandanna was chosen. The receiver
may ask for clarification on comments, but may not dialogue about
these comments—the idea is to focus on listening to the qualities/
attributes about them that are being presented. Once the bandanna
is given, the recipient may comment on the statements made, but
this is not necessary or expected.

As the process continues, it usually becomes obvious to the
group that they must consider each member so everyone ends up
with the "correct" bandanna. In some groups you may want to
punctuate this point as a facilitator, but quite often this is not necessary. Your role as a facilitator is to listen, be gatekeeper for unnec-
essary comments, and facilitate what group members have to offer.
I often focus on punctuating comments of group members that are
particularly meaningful for the recipient to hear.

Thoughts: The "richness" of the debriefing experience generally
occurs in the dialogue of why a particular bandanna goes to a particular person. As a facilitator, I have found it helpful to encourage

this process. Again, people may comment on the receipt of their "gift" bandanna, but it is not necessary.

In a recent research study about the long-term effects of adventure learning, I interviewed a past participant from a program in 1984. We were in her home, talking about what the experience meant to her, when she reached for the top drawer of her cabinet and pulled out a well-used bandanna. She said she could remember what the group had said about her in the debriefing experience (e.g., that she was a shining, bright member of the group who stood up for the group and what she believed was right, and that the power in her voice was radiant when she spoke and valued by the group). She stated that at that particular time in her life it was important to hear that feedback. She had kept her bandanna throughout the years and used it as a source of life perspective. Not only had she taken the bandanna with her on several backpacking trips, but also through moments of other life challenges.

References

Association for Experiential Education. (1992). *Ethical guidelines of the Therapeutic Adventure Professional Group (TAPG)*. Boulder, CO: Association for Experiential Education.

Atkins, S. & Murphy, K. (1993). Reflection: A review of the literature. *Journal of Advanced Nursing* 18, 1188-1192.

Berg, I. K. (1994). *Family based services: A solution-focused approach*. New York: W. W. Norton & Company.

Boud, D., Keough, R., & Walker, D. (1985). *Reflection: Turning experience into learning*. London: Kegan Page.

Boyd, E. & Fales, A. (1983). Reflective learning: Key to learning from experience. *Journal of Humanistic Psychology* 23(2), 99-117.

Caine, R.H. & Caine, G. (1994). *Making connection: Teaching and the human brain*. Menlo Park, CA: Addison-Wesley Publishing Company.

Cairn, R. (1991). Reflection: Learning from the service experience. In R. Cairn & J. Kielsmeier (Eds.). *Growing hope: A sourcebook on integrating youth service into the school curriculum*. Roseville, MN: National Youth Leadership Council.

Conrad, D. & Hedin, D. (1991). In R. Cairn & J. Kielsmeier (Eds.). *Growing hope: A sourcebook on integrating youth service into the school curriculum*. Roseville, MN: National Youth Leadership Council.

De la Harpe, B. & Radloff, A. (1997). Do first year students reflect on their learning? Why they should and how they can. Paper presented at the Annual Higher Education Research and Development Society of Australasia International Conference, Auckland, New Zealand.

Dewey, J. (1933). *How we think*. Boston, MA: D.C. Heath & Co., Publishers.

Dewey, J. (1938). *Experience in Education*, New York: Collier Books.

Fosnot, C.T. (1989). *Enquiring teachers, enquiring learners: A contructivist approach for teaching*. New York: Teachers College Press.

Frankl, V. (1984). *Man's search for meaning*. New York: Simon & Schuster, Inc.

Freire, P. (1984). *Pedagogy of the oppressed*. New York: The Continuum Publishing Corporation.

Gardner, H. (1993). *Multiple intelligences: The theory in practice.* New York: Basic Books.

Gass, M.A. & Gillis H.L. (1995a). CHANGES: An assessment model using adventure experiences. *Journal of Experiential Education* 18(1), 34-40.

Gass, M. A. & Gillis, H. L. (1995b). Constructing solutions in adventure therapy. *Journal of Experiential Education* 18 (2), 63-69.

Gillis, H. L., Gass, M. A., Bandoroff, S.; Rudolph, S., Clapp, C., & Nadler, R. (1991). Family adventure survey: Results and discussion. In C. Birmingham (Ed.). *Proceedings Journal of the 19th Annual AEE Conference.* Boulder, CO: Association for Experiential Education.

Hammel, H. (1986). How to design a debriefing session. *Journal of Experiential Education* 9(3), 20-25.

Kiser, D. J., Piercy, F. P., & Lipchik, E. (1993). The integration of emotion in solution-focused therapy. *Journal of Marital and Family Therapy* 19 (3), 235-244.

Kolb, D. (1984). *Experiential learning: Experience as the source of learning and development.* Englewood Cliffs, NJ: Prentice-Hall.

Luckner, J.L. & Nadler, R.S. (1997). *Processing the experience: Strategies to enhance and generalize learning.* Dubuque, IA: Kendall Hunt Publishing Company.

Oulette, G. (1991). In R. Cairn & J. Kielsmeier (Eds.). *Growing hope: A sourcebook on integrating youth service into the school curriculum.* Roseville, MN: National Youth Leadership Council.

Pfeiffer, J.W., & Jones, J.E. (1980). *The 1980 annual handbook for group facilitators,* San Diego: University Associates.

Piaget, J. (1965). *The Moral Judgment of the Child.* Translated by M. Gabain. New York: The Free Press.

Priest, S. (1988). The role of judgment, decision making, and problem solving for outdoor leaders. *Journal of Experiential Education* 12(3), 29-36.

Priest, S. and Gass, M. (1997a). *Effective leadership in adventure programming.* Champaign, IL: Human Kinetics Publishing.

Priest, S. & Gass, M. A. (1997b). An examination of "problem solving" verses "solution oriented" facilitation styles in a corporate setting. *Journal of Experiential Education* 20 (1), 34-39.

Priest, S., & Naismith, M. (1993). The debriefing funnel. *Journal of Adventure Education and Outdoor Leadership* 10(3), 20-22.

Quinsland, L.K., & Van Gindel, A. (1984). How to process experience. *Journal of Experiential Education* 7(2), 8-13.

Rhonke, K. (1984). *Silver bullets.* Hamilton, MA: Project Adventure.

Ringer, M. & Gillis, H. L. (1995). Managing psychological depth in adventure programming. *Journal of Experiential Education* 18 (1), 41-51.

Rossiter, K. (1999). *A survey of journal practices among faculty teaching outdoor education at institutions offering baccalaureate degree granting programs with specializations in outdoor education.* Unpublished master's thesis, University of New Hampshire, Durham.

Schoel, J., Prouty, D., & Radcliffe, P. (1988). *Islands of Healing: A guide to adventure-based counseling.* Dubuque, IA: Kendall/Hunt.

Schon, D. A. (1983). *The reflective practitioner: How professionals think in action.* New York: Basic Books, Inc.

Schon, D. A. (1987). *Educating the reflective practitioner.* San Francisco, CA: Jossey-Bass Publishers.

Sprinthall, N., Sprinthall, R., & Oja, S. (1994). *Educational psychology: A developmental approach.* New York: McGraw-Hill, Inc.

Williamson, J., & Gass, M.A. (1993). *Manual of program accreditation standards for adventure programs.* Boulder, CO: Association for Experiential Education.